P9-DVT-673
C A

The Idea of Canada

Letters to a Nation

David Johnston

Cloth edition published 2016

Signal is an imprint of McClelland & Stewart, a division of
Penguin Random House Canada Limited, a Penguin Random House Company

Library and Archives Canada Cataloguing in Publication
is available upon request

ISBN 978-0-7710-5077-0
eISBN 978-0-7710-5078-7

Book design by CS Richardson

Typeset in ITC Franklin Gothic & Adobe Caslon Pro
by McClelland & Stewart, Toronto
Printed and bound in the USA

McClelland & Stewart,
a division of Penguin Random House Canada Limited,
a Penguin Random House Company
www.penguinrandomhouse.ca

1 2 3 4 5 20 19 18 17 16

Penguin
Random
House

To my wife, Sharon, our five daughters,
and our twelve grandchildren who embody
our hopes for Canada.

Contents

Part Three: What Inspires Me

Introduction

Dear Reader,

Early in my life I landed on the notion that a mind exercised in the morning might, throughout the day, somehow stay more nimble than otherwise. History will likely prove this thesis wrong in my case, yet the presumption has often led me since university days to absorb myself in crafting two or three letters immediately after rising.

I have found over time that setting down a few thoughts – perhaps those hatched in conversation the evening prior or those that disturb my sleep in the dark hours – helps root me each day in the progress of ideas, affections, loyalties, and aspirations I have come to think of as my business in life.

My morning letters are typically either expressions of gratitude to those who have served their causes well, admiration for those who have pioneered new ways of thinking, or, when bold, encouragement to those embarking on uncertain adventures. The selfish benefit of these exercises is that I seem to understand each idea I begin with more vividly after writing about it than I did beforehand. As such, it seemed appropriate – even instinctive – to choose letters as a medium in which to explore the values, sensibilities, traditions, and achievements that make Canada unique. And so I did. Based on facts as I knew them.

I wrote some of these to friends and colleagues I know or knew well, and others to people and even groups of people I wish I knew better. Some were sent and some were not, often simply because their intended recipients had passed away.

I offer them here in all humility. As disparate as they might be in topic and tone, together they house the general set of realities that have shaped me, that consume me, and that inspire me to see Canada itself as an idea worthy of expression and searching for refinement. My hope is that perhaps by reading a few, you might help me do both.

Warmly,
David Johnston
Ottawa 2016

Foreword

There were three constants in our life growing up with our dad: driving, reading, and writing. He drove us all over the place – to our social activities, sports practices, hockey games, and, later on, to and from university when we needed to be dropped off or picked up, or just wanted to come home for a visit. He logged a lot of miles in our family station wagon. It never really crossed our minds that he had a day job beyond driving (often through the night). He was always there when we needed him. He would joke that the pay wasn't great but the company was pretty good.

The second constant was reading. He read to us in the evenings and on weekends from a very early age. Many of the stories he shared (C.S. Lewis's Narnia series, *The Secret Garden*, *Anne of Green Gables*, *The Hobbit*) helped shape our views and values growing up and initiated our understanding of the world beyond the communities we lived in. Our dad now continues the reading tradition with our children – who have always referred to him as Grampa Book.

The third constant was writing . . . and those who have had to interpret our dad's handwriting will be grateful that these letters can be so easily read in print!

When we went away to school and, as young adults, started to travel, our dad wrote to each of us, often every morning. We can't recall the number of letters he wrote but we do remember he always took the time to write. He would share thoughts and information on what was going on at work and at home, often with some passing wisdom on life. He wrote to connect with us and connect us to each other. Mostly he just wanted each of us to know that he loved us.

The only thing our father loves as much as his family is his country. So it is no surprise to us that he chose to share his passion and love for Canada by writing letters to Canadians. This country has given our parents so much, in particular the opportunity to build meaningful lives and careers. And in these last few years, the privileged vantage point, in their respective roles, to deepen their understanding of the country and expand the chance to give back.

Our dad is as principled, progressive, and loving as anyone we know. Each of us has benefited tremendously from our father-daughter road trips, his storytelling, and his letter writing. We know he shares these letters in the same spirit he shared letters with us – as a genuine expression of love and to highlight what makes this country so great – its people. These letters may inspire others to share their own reflections on our country with the people they love.

Deborah, Alexandra, Sharon (Jr.), Jenifer, and Sam Catherine Johnston

Part One

What Shapes Me

Who Am I, Anyway?

A simple answer to one boy's profound question.

To an unknown Inuit boy

Dear Young Friend,

Not a day has passed since we met that I haven't thought of you and the question you asked me. And I don't even know your name! Perhaps you've forgotten me? We met in your hometown. My journey to Repulse Bay, Nunavut, was one of my very first as governor general. When we saw each other at a community gathering, you asked me: "Who are you, anyway?" What a great question. I responded by telling you that I was the governor general. The more I've thought about your question, however, the more I've realized how incomplete my answer was. Being governor general is who I was at that exact moment, and the position is probably the last significant one I will hold during my career. Yet no kid in Canada ever grows up thinking, "Someday, I want to be governor general." A doctor or pro hockey player or prime minister, sure. But governor general?

So your question is a smart one – probably the most meaningful question one person can pose to another or one person can ask himself or herself. Let me try to answer it now. Who am I, anyway?

I'm Scottish-Irish-Canadian. My ancestors came to Canada from Scotland by way of Northern Ireland. They found struggle, sacrifice, and setbacks, like nearly all immigrants to our country. They also found opportunities – for themselves but more so for their descendants. I have done my best to seize and make the most of the many opportunities that have come my way.

I'm a small-town kid. Several generations after my father's ancestors settled in the Ottawa Valley, I was born in Sudbury, Ontario, and grew up in Sault Ste. Marie. When I was growing up there, the Soo was a natural resources town – steel, lumber, pulp and paper. It was remote and isolated – a place most people passed through on the way to somewhere else – but it was also safe and secure. My father ran a hardware store, my mother our home. My schools nurtured my curiosity, and my community gave me support. I began after-school work at age nine and learned the heady satisfaction of self-reliance.

I'm a student-athlete. For me, the two have always gone together. I played hockey in the winter, baseball in the summer, and football in the fall – all of them at school, on city league teams, and in countless pickup games with my friends. I also worked hard at school, because I realized early that an education opened many doors – a strong education was my ticket to a rewarding career and fulfilling life. I was fortunate to be a good enough athlete and a good enough student to earn a scholarship from Harvard University. In the late 1950s, the school had started looking for students from places other than blueblood families of the northeast United States – especially young men who excelled in their studies and in a sport. Bill Bender, Dean of Admissions for Harvard College, unleashed Harvard's alumni to find these new "diamonds in the rough." I was amongst the roughest of these, contacted in grade 10 in my high school in Sault Ste. Marie by a Harvard alumnus in Minnesota. Thus began my love affair with Harvard.

I played hockey at Harvard for four years and was selected to the All-American team in the last two and subsequently named to Harvard's Athletic Hall of Fame. Our team during those years was the best in our conference and one of the top in the country. I worked equally hard as a student as I did as an athlete, graduating magna cum laude and earning a scholarship to study law at the University of Cambridge in Great Britain. I returned home to Canada eventually – to Queen's University – to finish my student days and earn a law degree.

I'm a lawyer and a teacher. Again, the two go hand in hand for me. I love the law. Our laws – arrived at by our legislators and interpreted by our judges – are the bedrock on which our country rests. Our laws also enable us to advance closer and closer to justice – an elusive goal but one we should never cease trying to reach. I never practised law, though. I taught it. I was a law professor and a law school dean. These roles enabled me to gain the knowledge and experiences I needed to become a university president, which I was for twenty-seven years. Being a student for some years and a university teacher, dean, and executive for many more enabled me to learn plenty about the idea of education and the ways in which education is practised in Canada and around the world. Reaching out to schools in other countries to help students and teachers exchange and expand knowledge was a joyful and fulfilling preoccupation of mine that continues to this day.

I'm a public servant. I have served on task forces, inquiries, round tables, and commissions established by provincial and federal governments. And I carried out the duties of governor general for five years and will do so for another two years until after Canada's 150th birthday in the summer of 2017. I assumed all these roles because I believe public service to be an honourable calling and sacred duty. I have been blessed to live, work, and raise a family in this country. Public service is a way for me to make a small measure of return to the country that has given me so much. I will always answer my country's call to service eagerly and gratefully.

I'm a husband, father, and grandfather. (I've saved the best for last.) I married my childhood sweetheart. I met Sharon when she was thirteen years old and I was fourteen. Although we were separated for long stretches while I attended university, I think we were destined to be together for life. She has helped me have a fulfilling career, contributing to my roles as university dean and executive, as well as governor general. She has also had the energy, intelligence, and determination to earn a doctorate in rehabilitation medicine and to run her own business. On top of all that, she has recently published her first novel, based on her grandmother's life. She is now working on a second, about her mother, and plans a third, which will be about the two of us and our children. She's an incredible woman. Together, we have raised five daughters. Everything truly worth learning in life I have come to understand from them. They are more than children; they are my inspiration every day. I'm also a grandfather of twelve. They keep me young – not merely by helping me stay active but also by enabling me to view our world through their eyes. I hope one day you will find the kind of joy and wisdom they have granted me.

When we met in Repulse Bay, you asked me: "Who are you, anyway?" That's my answer – for now, anyway.

Your friend,
David

Mr. Johnston's friend is an eight-year-old Inuit boy he met on one of his first visits outside Ottawa as governor general. The happy, curious youngster found himself standing next to Mr. Johnston at a start of Repulse Bay's Terry Fox charity run. The runs, which are held in more than 100 countries around the world, raise money for cancer research. Mr. Johnston and his family have participated in them for more than three decades. The Repulse Bay Terry Fox run is the most northerly version of the run in the world. The brief conversation between Mr. Johnston and the boy went like this:

“Who are you, anyway?”

“I’m the governor general.”

“What’s your name, anyway?”

“My name is David.”

“How old are you, anyway, David?”

“I’m seventy years old.”

“Seventy! I didn’t think anybody could get that old, anyway.”

When Mr. Johnston had finished the five-kilometre run, he spotted the boy in the crowd, walked up to him, poked him gently in the shoulder, smiled, and said, “Not dead yet, anyway.”

What Champlain Teaches

Three lessons from Canada's first public servant.

To Janice Charette

Dear Janice,

The Right Honourable Georges Vanier, Canada's nineteenth governor general, said that he knew of no occupation more noble than service and no calling higher than service of the public. I agree. I have profound respect for you and for the work you and your colleagues in Canada's public service do on behalf of our country and its citizens. I have seen the excellence of Canadian public servants first-hand when I chaired, over a number of years, a dozen or so different national or provincial task forces such as the National Roundtable on the Environment and the Economy, Information Highway Advisory Council, National Broadband Task Force, Committee on Information

Systems for the Environment, and the National Advisory Committee on Online Learning. On a much more personal note, all the important things in my life I've learned from public servants – my five children. They are highly accomplished women in the public service and exemplars of professionalism, dedication, and selflessness. They share these virtues with the men and women of Canada's public service. It's no secret that these professionals and the institution they represent now face unprecedented challenges. Foremost among them is the fact that Canada's future can no longer be viewed in isolation – as maybe it once could be. Our future will be influenced profoundly by globalization – on the interaction we have with the world and the world has with us. This increasingly integrated world confronts us in Canada with problems and opportunities that were little known to past generations of Canadians. On top of that, most problems are becoming more complex because our understanding of them grows more nuanced, and because the number of people affected by them increases. Our ultimate success in tackling any problem we face will depend on how we acquire, analyze, and apply relevant knowledge. In education, we must have equality of opportunity and excellence too. The value of knowledge always depends on how we use it. Canada can be a global knowledge leader – a smart nation, an Athens to the new Rome – but our efforts must always be directed toward helping people realize their true potential as individuals and, in our doing so, we enrich the lives of us all. We must become smarter so we can be more caring.

Service that enhances the public good must remain a constant influence on everything you and the public service do. I urge you to keep this affirmation in the forefront of your mind and at the heart of your actions as you process changes called for by your political masters, as you manage the integration of advances brought by technological innovation, as you set standards for new workers, and as you prepare organizations to overcome anticipated and unanticipated obstacles. As you tackle these modern-day challenges, I recommend that you and all public servants draw inspiration from Samuel de Champlain. A public servant and the first governor – in all but name – of what we now call Canada, Champlain is misunderstood. He has been portrayed as a great discoverer and conquistador – and he was, without a doubt, a product of his time – but he was at his core an innovator who dedicated his life to building a society based on diversity, tolerance, inclusiveness, peace, and the rule of law – values that underpin our country to this day. Indeed, Champlain's vision of what would become Canada is just as relevant today as it was four centuries ago, and Canada's public servants can gain many valuable insights from him about leadership in times of change and instability.

As an explorer, Champlain was quick to acknowledge his total dependence on the people around him. He meticulously gathered information on the geography and society of the New World from Basque whalers and fishermen and from members of local Aboriginal tribes. The Settlement of Port Royal would not have survived its first winter in 1608 were it not for the generous help of its Aboriginal neighbours. Champlain studied the languages of a number of First Nations so he could learn from them directly. He befriended tribes with which he came into contact. He was also a practitioner of religious tolerance, having had to convert in his youth from protestant Huguenot to Catholic to save his own life. As a leader, Champlain was a careful student of earlier attempts at colonization, applying lessons of history to his own experience. For instance, he learned that he required a careful blend of men and women from divergent walks of life to build a thriving community. This knowledge made him sensitive to the differences of the people he brought to New France. Champlain also appreciated the value of justice and rule of law – both at the time in short supply in colonial lands and among colonial leaders. These principles enabled Champlain to institute a regime of order and fairness that validated his authority in the minds of his people. It was a giant leap forward. Before Champlain's leadership, the French had failed on six occasions to set up a permanent settlement in North America. As a public servant, Champlain knew that he was immediately accountable to those he led (for survival) and to his patron, King Henry IV of France (for planting a secure foothold on the continent). Yet he knew also that ultimate triumph in the New World required him to look beyond this pressing calling to account and – in the words of biographer David Hackett Fischer – to prepare for the unexpected in a world of uncertainty, learn how to make sound judgements on the basis of imperfect knowledge, and take a broad view and plan for the long run.

Just as he learned from the experiences of others, I ask you to ponder three lessons from Champlain's life in New France. One, rely on the knowledge and expertise of the people around you. Command and control methods of managing have had their day in the sun. Successful leaders and high-performance managers today recognize and will into the future that their organizations' success depends on those around them. Two, share vital information and responsibilities widely and authorize others to use them to generate new knowledge, find solutions, and become vigorous leaders in their own right. Our problems are daunting, but the possibilities for innovation, experimentation, and problem-solving are even greater if we share vital information with all those in our organizations; empower them to use that information to experiment, innovate, and approach public-sector activities as entrepreneurs; and reward them for success while urging them to learn from their failures. When trust is strong, anything is possible. When trust is lost, it is rarely regained. (As Mark Carney, former governor of the Bank of Canada and now the Bank of England's governor, once observed, "Trust comes in on foot and goes out in a Ferrari.") And three, take calculated risks rather than forgo needed action merely because risks exist. Thomas Homer-Dixon – in his 2010 Manion Lecture to public servants – likened successful leaders to gardeners who establish conditions for growth and creativity. As any gardener can tell you, though, not all experiments work out. Allowing for the possibility of short-term failure is an essential precondition for successful innovations and a defining characteristic of smart organizations and, indeed, smart nations. Therein lies the secret. We can talk all we want about innovation, experimentation, and risk-taking in government, but if we punish those whose bold ideas don't pan out, we will stifle any genuine spirit of innovation in the public service. Accountability and rigour in operations are vital. Yet we need accountability in the public service that won't drive out entrepreneurship and risk-taking. We must learn, therefore, to differentiate between mistakes made through experimentation – which we encourage – and those made in error, which will occur from time to time and which we must address through early recognition and by learning from our setbacks.

You serve as the exemplar for the women and men you lead. You must be the vanguard of an open, knowledge-based, empowered spirit within departments and agencies of the public service. Be open with all your people. Encourage experimentation. Nurture leaders. Sanction sensible risks. Reward success, yet never condemn honourable efforts that come up short. While this approach is needed now, its biggest payoff will come in the near future. The smartest, most ambitious young people in our country will consider careers in the public service only if they are free to experiment, innovate, and lead. The way to attract them isn't by simply lowering cubicle walls, incorporating fitness centres within office buildings, or integrating smartphones and tablets into workplace communications systems. Canada's public service must attract our country's most talented new workers and thinkers by giving them genuine authority to wield, real opportunities to pursue, vexing challenges to overcome, and inspiring goals to achieve.

I'm gladdened that some are heeding this call. When I was president of the University of Waterloo, Kevin Lynch – who was clerk of the Privy Council at the time – asked if our school would set up a job fair in the Waterloo area. He was concerned about the eroding ability of the public service to attract the most qualified candidates. (How ironic is it that Canada is working with countries such as Mongolia to bolster the quality of its public service while we have been hollowing out our own?) For two days, some eighty deputy ministers and assistant deputy ministers came to Waterloo to speak about jobs in the public service and to interview potential candidates. It was an outstanding success. More than a thousand students from the University of Waterloo and surrounding schools attended, many of whom had no prior interest in the public service. I buttonholed a number of the students afterward and they told me how they were thunderstruck by three revelations: the idealism of serving the public, the variety of careers that they could pursue in the public service, and the breadth of responsibility given so early to young public servants. I urge you to stay focused on this winning approach. This will enable Canada's public service to play its part in realizing the smart, caring Canada Champlain dreamed of more than four hundred years ago and the smarter, more caring Canada all of us dream of today.

Thank you for serving Canada.
David

Janice Charette is Clerk of the Privy Council and Secretary to the Cabinet. The top non-political official in the Government of Canada, the Clerk fulfills three primary functions. The Clerk gives advice and support to the Prime Minister on policies and operations related to the Government of Canada. As Secretary to the Cabinet, the Clerk ensures the continuity of government between successive administrations, keeps custody of the records of previous administrations, and enables the government of the day to understand and recognize the established conventions of Canada's constitutional monarchy. As head of the federal public service, the Clerk makes sure the Government of Canada has the policies, managers, and professionals it needs to design and deliver programs and services to Canadians.

You Can't Learn on an Empty Stomach

A lesson to an educator on humility.

To Jacline Nyman

Dear Jacline,

You're never too old or too accomplished to receive a lesson in humility. I learned a valuable one early in the 1980s when I co-chaired the United Way's annual fundraising campaign in Montreal.

Until then – I'm still chagrined to admit – I had not really known my city and I had not really known my profession. I lived in an affluent neighbourhood and worked at McGill University as principal. And yet I never realized the depth of need in places beyond the campus or outside my family's immediate community. In particular, I never realized one out of every four boys in East Montreal at age five had never read a book. I never realized schoolchildren there didn't have quiet places of their own where they could do their homework. I especially never realized many of them came to school hungry and malnourished.

I was astonished! How could I as a Montrealer live in a city with so much need and not be aware of it? How could I as an educator of young men and women talk about the latest advances in teaching methods and tools and not understand that many youngsters in my city couldn't engage their minds when all they were thinking about was the ache in their stomachs?

Your organization and others like yours were aware and responded with school breakfast and lunch programs that to this day help young students reach their full potential in the classroom. On a lesser yet more personal note, your organization helped teach this Montreal educator about his city and his profession, and in doing so gave me a much-needed lesson in humility.

For that, I thank you.
David

Jacline Nyman is president and chief executive officer of United Way Centraide Canada.

Going the Wrong Way

What bravery says about our country.

To Kevin Vickers

Dear Kevin,

A photograph is displayed prominently at the Royal Canadian Mounted Police Academy in Regina. The photo captures a moment in time during an emergency at an unidentified school. While terrified students and teachers stream out of the building, one person moves against the tide, heading with purpose toward the source of danger. When I visited the academy, I looked at the photo for a long time – that one man in particular. We don't know who he is. He wears the uniform of the RCMP, but we can't see his face. I call him "the wrong-way guy." Faceless, anonymous, unknown, the wrong-way guy to me stands for all the men and women in our country who rush toward danger while the rest of us head the other way.

I have encountered many wrong-way guys and gals as governor general. I met dozens of them at Rideau Hall ceremonies at which Canada honoured them for their acts of exceptional bravery. They were military personnel, first responders, and Canadians who wore no uniform. I saw their faces, learned their names, shook their hands, heard their stories, and met their families. I was humbled continually by all these selfless men and women.

I saw wrong-way guys and gals in action in Resolute Bay on the Northwest Passage when my wife, Sharon, and I visited Nunavut. While I was touring the Canadian Armed Forces Arctic Training Facility at the time of Operation Nanook, preparing for a mock commercial airline crash, the real thing happened! A passenger plane had crashed one kilometre from the runway and two kilometres from where we were having lunch in the mess tent. Sharon and I watched in awe as the men and women of Joint Task Force North responded swiftly and with supreme professionalism to the emergency, sending rescue and medical personnel into the most unforgiving region in the country. And then, when that was over, the small community of six hundred expressed their grief and celebrated the lives of the twelve who perished in the crash with a worship service conducted by the military padre in English, French, and Inuktitut.

I witnessed bravery of a different sort in Moncton at the memorial service for RCMP Constable Douglas Larche and his two colleagues killed on duty. At the conclusion of the service, I came to say goodbye to Doug and his wife Nadine's three young daughters: Mia, Lauren, and Alexandra. All three wore hats: Mia, the eldest, wore her father's Stetson; Lauren, the middle child, wore the Stetson of RCMP Commissioner Bob Paulson; and Alexandra, the youngest, had on the Royal Canadian Navy peaked cap of her officer uncle. As I left them, they saluted me in unison. Theirs was an act of respect their father no doubt had taught them and an unmistakable sign of their courage to carry on in spite of the unspeakable tragedy that had befallen their family.

And of course, all Canadians beheld the bravery of many wrong-way guys and gals on October 22, 2014. We learned of the heroism of six at the National War Memorial, where many rushed to help and comfort a mortally wounded Nathan Cirillo as the echo and odour of gunfire were fresh in the air. We heard tell of many others on Parliament Hill – RCMP and House of Commons security personnel – who made sure the murderer of Corporal Cirillo would kill no further. You in particular that day showed us that wrong-way guys and gals are professionals – paramedics, firefighters, police officers, military and security personnel who are trained to respond with skill, with speed, and without fail. That day also showed us that wrong-way guys and gals are what I call extraordinary ordinary Canadians. Acts of bravery are often carried out by men and women who might never have assumed they had what it took to be brave; who might never have supposed they could act without a moment's hesitation; who might never have believed they could move ahead without a thought for themselves; and who might never have expected they could risk all they had, regardless of whether they were adequately trained, equipped, or prepared. Extraordinary ordinary Canadians show us as well that acts of bravery are not performed solely on epic battlefields or during legendary campaigns. Bravery often unfolds in our own backyards, in our homes, at our workplaces, in our cars and on our streets, at the beach, or on familiar rivers, lakes, and seas.

The many examples of bravery I encountered as governor general compelled me to reflect often on the source of such bravery. Most wrong-way guys and gals risk their lives to preserve the lives of others and then afterward insist they are no heroes. I think there is something profound about this modesty, and that the deep humility of those who act so dauntlessly points us to the true nature of bravery. I'm convinced bravery comes from a deep-seated, sacrificial love that drives away fear, a pure form of love that enables someone to look beyond his or her limitations, to remain on his or her guard, to stand firm, determined, and composed even in the midst of a crisis. St. Augustine, a philosopher who lived in the late fourth century, wrote: "What does love look like? It has the hands to help others. It has the feet to hasten to the poor and needy. It has the eyes to see misery and want. It has the ears to hear the sighs and sorrows of men." Wrong-way guys and gals use their hands to shield the innocent, protecting them from attacks, to break through doors and windows, and to cut confining straps, releasing the trapped from danger. Their feet charge into harm's way, through flames and noxious fumes, pulling the injured and reluctant to safety, and run into water, kicking against currents, tides, and ice floes to keep the sinking afloat. Their eyes spot the lost in the wilderness; their ears hear the desperate cries for help. In all these ways, wrong-way guys and gals show the most genuine form of love anyone ever possibly could for someone else. They were prepared to put their lives in the balance to preserve another. They risked everything they had so that someone else might have the chance to see another day. Service is love made real.

These many examples of bravery also demanded that I consider what such bravery says about our country. I think it says we have built something very special in this country that is worth preserving – to the point that many risk their very lives to do so. I think it says we understand that many of our country's most precious values – the rule of law, the protection of human rights, the respect for others (especially the "different others"), we call inclusiveness, and an intrinsic sense of fairness that sees us care for the health and well-being of others – would be severely compromised without the willingness of many to act bravely. And I think it says we have a desire to make this country even better, and that – paradoxically yet gloriously – going the wrong way moves us closer to becoming the more caring nation we all want Canada to be.

With thanks,
David

Kevin Vickers is Canada's ambassador to Ireland. Prior to assuming his current role, he served as an RCMP officer and then as Sergeant-at-Arms of the House of Commons of Canada, a post in which he was responsible for the safety and security of the Parliament Buildings. Ambassador Vickers played a determinant role in ending the October 22, 2014, shootings at Parliament Hill when he and his colleagues from the House of Commons and RCMP officers confronted and killed the gunman who shot and killed Corporal Nathan Cirillo, a ceremonial guard at the National War Memorial, and who shot and wounded a House of Commons constable at the Peace Tower entrance of the Centre Block.

The Zen of Licking Stamps

Letters recognize, applaud, and build on the positive.

To all young leaders

Dear young leaders,

Many people ask me to share with them my thoughts about leadership and, more specifically, what goes into being an effective leader. (I guess that happens to you when you start looking as old as I do.) I tell these people, as I'm telling you now, that one fundamental element of my leadership equation is a simple one: the best leaders build on the positive and manage the negative. This statement is easy to understand: accentuate all the good things happening around you in whatever group of people you lead, and take action to eliminate the harmful things going on, or at least mitigate them to lessen the harm.

Writing letters is the best way I know of to reinforce the positive. The first thing I do when I arrive at my office and sit down at my desk each morning is to write a few. I try to get these letters done before the events of the unfolding day take over. The letters I write usually go to men and women I have met at several events I've often attended the day or evening before. While these people and events are fresh in my mind, I send a few words of thanks for an exciting speech delivered or generous act made or smart decision taken. The simple human act of writing shows people you recognize and applaud their achievements and, in doing so, encourages them to build on these accomplishments to do even more.

Writing letters is appropriate for any leader who is at the head of a group of people – whether that group is a business, a department in a large organization, or even a family. That's how I started. I wrote a letter home to my parents every Sunday while I was away at school. I extended the practice while I was at school in England, writing my fiancée, and now wife, Sharon, every day. When our first daughter went away to school, I made a habit of writing to her regularly. These were the days before electronic mail. When her four younger sisters started leaving home for school, I began to write them too. Typically, each work-day morning I would write one letter to them all and send copies. As they grew older, I would occasionally write a separate postscript to one or more. At any given time, two of the girls would ignore my letters. "There goes Dad babbling on again," I imagine they said to themselves. Two others would read them casually, perhaps thinking, "Oh, that's interesting."

To one daughter, however, the letter would be quite meaningful at that particular time. And the daughter who drew meaning from the letter would change over time. Writing these and all other letters was always meaningful to me and remains so.

Over time, my circle of recipients expanded well beyond my family. I was reminded of my penchant for letter writing – and my increasingly indecipherable handwriting – at the farewell party for Wally Crowston, long-time dean of the management school at McGill University, where I served as principal for fifteen years. When it came time for Wally's speech, he brought before those assembled a large box, which he opened to reveal dozens and dozens of letters. He said they were all the notes he had received from the boss over the years. He continued to say that while he could never make out the handwriting enough to understand them, he had always chosen to believe they were full of praise.

They probably were, or mostly all of them were. That's how you lead – in business, in any large organization, in a family, in life. Use letters to stress the positive. Use other methods – visits, phone calls, meetings – to manage the negative. It's an axiom I've lived by and led by for much of my life. I encourage you, as men and women who are just starting to lead, to carve out some time each morning to write a letter or two to people you want to recognize, applaud, and encourage to build on their achievements. The recipient and the writer will both be better for it.

Encouragingly yours,
David

Letters can be effective even when one's penmanship is lacking. All readers, including the emerging leaders reading this letter, should be grateful that the author did not publish these letters in his original longhand. In fact, his marvellous executive assistant, Nicole, frequently includes a typed transcript to mitigate all mystery.

Chemistry Not Math

What Mother Teresa taught me about giving.

To Ian Bird

Dear Ian,

Even the smallest act of giving can change someone's life, if not the world. You're aware of this truth. As governor general, I used it to inspire our charitable campaign – My Giving Moment. I must confess, however, realization about giving has been a continuous journey in my life. And strangely enough, a magician was the one who enabled me to see the light in its most illuminating form.

Many years ago, Mother Teresa – the famed nun who founded the Missionaries of Charity – made her first visit to Canada to share with Canadians the story of her work to help the dying, sick, and destitute of Calcutta. An editorial in one of our country's major newspapers lauded her intentions yet despaired at the futility of her efforts. Her work was described as a drop of hope in an ocean of despair. What was the point, the paper proclaimed, in helping a mere several hundreds of people in a city of millions in a country of hundreds of millions, most of whom lived in desperate poverty?

This opinion troubled me. I knew in my heart it was wrong, but my brain couldn't identify precisely the reason why until months later – at a children's birthday party, of all places. The star attraction at these neighbourhood parties was a magician. The famed illusionist was really Andy MacFarlane, the dean of journalism at Western University. I was dean of the law school at the time. My competitive spirit inspired me to attend the next celebration. My children, aged two to nine at the time, had criticized the entertainment I provided at their parties. "Why can't you put on a magic show like Dean MacFarlane," they would plead, "instead of telling us ghost stories that aren't scary and that none of the kids believe?"

So I attended the next birthday party at Andy's home, and there I witnessed MacFarlane the Magnificent, clad in a crimson silk shirt with billowing sleeves and a long, dark cape. After several nifty card tricks and coin manipulations, the magnificent one declared he was now ready to present his most amazing illusion. He held up a glass of water and announced that he would turn water into wine. With his cape shielding the kids' view but not mine, Andy pulled an eyedropper from one of his flowing sleeves and squeezed a drop of red food colouring into the glass. He then uttered the magic word "Abracadabra," turned around, swirled the water in the glass, and the kids all watched in amazement as it slowly changed from clear to a lovely rose-hued liquid.

I also experienced an epiphany – but for a different reason. I realized then that the newspaper editorial had wholly misinterpreted Mother Teresa's work with a few destitute hundred in Calcutta. The paper's editorial writer had approached this work from a mathematical viewpoint when the writer should have seen the matter from its true perspective – chemistry. By improving the lives of even a few women and their families, Mother Teresa was altering the very nature of the glass of water, not adding to or subtracting from it, and by transforming it in her small way, she was catalyzing others – those she helped and those inspired by her example – to make small transformative acts of their own.

Giving is chemistry not math, or perhaps it is math plus chemistry; even one small act of giving can reshape someone's life, if not the world.

A fellow chemist,
David

Ian Bird is president of the Community Foundations of Canada, an organization that connects and supports 193 local community foundations across the country. Inspired by Mr. Johnston's appeal to Canadians to create a smart and caring nation, the Community Foundations of Canada, with the 193 individual foundations, has helped many community foundations set up special Smart and Caring Community Funds. Ian is also founding executive director of the Rideau Hall Foundation. An independent, non-political charitable organization, the Rideau Hall Foundation works with the Office of the Governor General on programs that enable Canadians to build a smarter, more caring country by giving. My Giving Moment and Queen Elizabeth II Diamond Jubilee Scholarships are two notable programs of the Rideau Hall Foundation.

Adversarial Allies

Exchanging ideas about justice with Mexico.

To Enrique Peña Nieto

Dear Enrique,

Justice is best guaranteed by democratic values and institutions. I had this truth in mind, along with a buoyant sense of optimism, when I represented Canada at your 2012 inauguration as president of Mexico. I was heartened to hear so much of your installation speech devoted to shining a bright light on the importance of democratic institutions, the protection of basic rights and freedoms, and the creation of a legal system centred on the constant, relentless pursuit of justice. Inspired by your words, the people of Mexico are renewing this pursuit. They understand that the rule of law and the never-ending advance toward justice are what make us free and secure as citizens.

They know that these virtues enable us to achieve our potential as human beings and as whole societies. And they know all too well – better than most people – the insecurity, instability, and fear that arise when a country's justice system is corrupted by intimidation, greed, and violence.

As I mentioned to you when we talked at your inauguration, I am delighted that Mexico is replacing its existing inquisitorial judicial system for criminal justice with an adversarial system similar to Canada's – the goal being to reduce corruption and strengthen accountability, transparency, and democratic rights in your country. As you know, the Western world's two main legal frameworks for criminal justice are known as the adversarial, or common law, system and the inquisitorial, or civil law, system. The inquisitorial system is premised on the notion that an independent officer of the state, whether a judge or a prosecutor, is the best person to seek and find the truth. Proceedings are conducted largely by paper and behind closed doors, with judges issuing verdicts based on all the evidence that has been collected and presented to them. In contrast, the adversarial system is based on the notion that judges are apt to lose their neutrality if they investigate the cases they try. The truth is most likely to surface where opposing counsels present their cases orally and publicly in court, often before a jury of ordinary citizens. In doing so, each counsel tries to convince an impartial judge or jury, possessed of no prior knowledge of the case, his or her version of events is true, while trying to cast doubt or find errors or incompleteness in the other side's evidence. The prosecutor's task is to present – vigorously and fairly – all relevant and admissible evidence to a judge or jury and let them decide the outcome. Importantly, proceedings in an adversarial system must be open and transparent, inspiring public confidence and reducing fear of corruption or unfairness. Another significant difference between the two models concerns what is considered admissible evidence. In an inquisitorial system, police do not have to follow the same strict procedures as in an adversarial system when gathering evidence – meaning that evidence, no matter how it is obtained, is considered admissible. By contrast, judges in an adversarial system look at evidence to determine whether it has been gathered in accordance with the law and prosecutors must disclose all relevant evidence to the defence. Judges have the power to exclude the evidence from the trial proceedings if they conclude it was obtained illegally or is unfairly prejudiced. In short, the ends do not necessarily justify the means.

The challenges of Mexico's sweeping judicial reform are daunting. You know full well the magnitude of the task. Many powerful, entrenched interests – within the system and without – would like nothing better than to preserve the status quo. I've learned that no one person or group of people should tackle great tasks alone. Great allies are essential. Mexicans have specifically sought out Canadian advice and assistance to speed and strengthen their process of reform. My eldest daughter, who works as a lawyer with the Public Prosecution Service of Canada, is part of a legal team that has been training prosecutors and developing guidelines in five Mexican states with the hope of contributing to a fairer, more accountable and transparent criminal justice system that inspires public confidence. In total, she has made eleven visits of this kind not only to Mexico but also elsewhere in Latin America, having trained prosecutors, public defenders, and judges in Chile and Colombia.

Canadians are also helping Mexico's law schools train the next generation of Mexican lawyers. Luis Fernando Pérez Hurtado, the president of the non-governmental Centre for the Study of Teaching and Learning of Law, spent six months in Canada studying the law curriculum of the University of Ottawa. With the support of the Anti-Crime Capacity Building Program of Foreign Affairs, Trade and Development Canada, the centre is also working with Mexican law schools to convert their curricula to reflect the new adversarial legal system. Having been a student, professor, and dean of law for many years, I have witnessed up close how legal education can support the practice of law and move societies closer to justice. By helping Mexican law faculties adapt to the reform and work in symbiosis with lawyers, judges, and officials, Canadians are making a real contribution to the pursuit of justice in Mexico. These partnerships are powerful examples of what I refer to as the diplomacy of knowledge – men and women working together across disciplines and borders to uncover, share, and refine knowledge to improve the human condition. As someone who cares deeply about justice and the rule of law, I am thrilled Mexico's judicial reformers are drawing insights and lessons from the criminal process used in Canada. My country gets plenty out of the partnership, too. While Canada's criminal justice system has a well-deserved reputation for transparency, accountability, and impartiality, ours is nonetheless imperfect and in need of constant evaluation and improvement. As the Honourable David Paciocco of the Ontario Court of Justice pointed out while taking part in a Canadian delegation to Mexico, the judicial reform taking place in Mexico offers Canadians an excellent opportunity to reaffirm our own commitment to move closer to justice. I am especially pleased we are working as partners to improve our systems of justice. This is but one of many instances where our association through NAFTA enhances the lives of both our peoples. It is also a strong signal we can do more in other spheres.

Just as Canada's legal system is founded on the notion that truth will surface where opposing counsels present their cases orally in court, I believe the exchange of ideas and experiences between Canada and Mexico can strengthen our democratic institutions and lead to greater justice and fairness for all. As close friends and partners in North America, we must strive for nothing less.

Yours in partnership,
David

Enrique Peña Nieto is the fifty-seventh president of Mexico. Mr. Johnston represented Canada at President Peña Nieto's inauguration, following which the two men had the opportunity to discuss many subjects, including reform of Mexico's criminal justice system and the work our two countries could undertake to further that reform.

Journey to Wellness

One woman's response to mental illness.

To Clara Hughes

Dear Clara,

I hesitate to write you this letter – for one simple reason: I'm afraid you won't have time to read it! The number and range of your activities and your capacity to push your physical and emotional limits on behalf of our country and its people staggers me. And I'm someone who not only has a pretty demanding schedule but also stays active because I appreciate the benefits of exercising to body and mind.

Yet I feel compelled to write. Meeting you to celebrate the conclusion of Clara's Big Ride in Arnprior and then on Parliament Hill and at Rideau Hall was a joy for me – just as it was for the many thousands of people who came out to see you and cheer you on. I was delighted to be a part of your team of riders for a short time. Although I'm an avid athlete, my mind boggles at what you accomplished during your ride through every province and territory. As you said with such eloquence at the time, while you expected your ride to be a physical ordeal (you worked every day from 3:30 in the morning till nine at night for 110 days straight), you never anticipated it being such an emotionally taxing one as well. You met thousands of people and listened to their stories. You heard them speak of the pain that so many are suffering and of our failure as a people to ensure they receive the support and care that is their right as Canadians. From what you've said, it's clear that this experience produced a pain in you as well – a deep feeling of distress at the work that remains for us all.

Take heart. Your efforts to get people talking and listening about mental illness have been a godsend for many Canadians. I'm one of them. My understanding of and therefore empathy toward people suffering from mental illnesses was typical of many Canadians. I didn't realize how many suffered and how many did so silently. As a result of your tireless efforts and selfless example, I've learned deeply about the human side of mental illness, especially the stigma that people living with mental illnesses are forced to bear. I've also learned that physical health is only one half of total wellness. Mental health is just as important as physical fitness and should be promoted by our country and sought after by our people with equal energy and devotion. And I've learned that achievement in other aspects of life – in your case, athletic success at the highest level – is no safeguard against the crippling effects of mental illness.

Nor is professional achievement, as the experience of William Kurelek makes clear. The famed Canadian artist suffered from schizophrenia, and he reflected and tried to come to grips with his illness through his art. In this way, he was an early practitioner of art as therapy. His series of six paintings titled *The Ukrainian Pioneer* has long been on display in the entrance hall at Rideau Hall. I see these works of art often and use these occasions to deepen my understanding of not only our country but also the man and his struggle with mental illness. These paintings also spurred Sharon to organize an evening at Rideau Hall called "The Happening" to screen *William Kurelek's The Maze*, a documentary film that explores Kurelek's struggles through his paintings, including *The Maze*, which is his depiction of the inside of his skull in the midst of his madness. We were all delighted that you could join us that evening.

Your life and that of Kurelek shows us that mental illness does not discriminate. It can affect anyone, regardless of age, race, gender, or culture. Its impact is felt by family, friends, and colleagues – by nearly every Canadian – in some way. And this fact will not change until we work together to improve our collective well-being. How do we achieve this goal? You've shown us one important way: through education. We must inform ourselves in order to help others. The more knowledge we have, the better we will be able to help those in need. And this process starts in our schools, by encouraging young people to think differently. We must urge them – and everyone, in fact – to speak up and to listen closely, to get involved and involve others, to seek help, and to recognize when someone needs help. We must not maintain silence – not when people are suffering, not when people's lives are at risk. We can improve lives, and even save them, if we simply make the effort.

You and William Kurelek are Canadian icons – heroes to many. You have also told us that so-called ordinary people have roles. Each of us has a responsibility to see the signs of mental illness in our families, friends, and peers and to help them to confront mental illness like a physical illness: identify, get help, and stick with the treatment to heal. In this way, we create *"ordinary"* heroes. God knows, Clara, you have made the effort to create heroes. Yet, as even you admitted at the end of your triumphant ride, we still have a long way to go to end the stigma of mental illness and ensure all those who suffer get the support and treatment they deserve and the courage to complete it. Thanks to you, though, our journey to wellness is a little shorter than before.

Thank you,
David

Clara Hughes is one of Canada's most distinguished and decorated athletes. A cyclist and speed skater, she competed in six Olympic Games – the 1996, 2000, and 2012 Summer Games, and the 2002, 2006, and 2010 Winter Games. An officer of the Order of Canada and member of Canada's Sports Hall of Fame, she is the only Canadian to win medals in both versions of the games and the only person to win multiple medals in both. In 2014, Clara undertook Clara's Big Ride, a 12,000-kilometre, 110-day cycling journey that saw her travel through every province and territory, visiting 95 communities and 80 schools, and attending more than 260 public events. She used the ride to speak with Canadians about mental illness, aiming to reduce the stigma associated with these illnesses. At one of the final events of Clara's journey, Mr. Johnston presented her with the Meritorious Service Cross, Civilian Division – a high award to recognize the particular actions she has taken to bring great benefit and honour to Canada.

Astounding Science Fiction

My big regret.

To Val O'Donovan

Dear Val,

When chatting about innovation with a group of friends the other day, I mentioned your name and your influence in making Canada a global leader in satellite communications technology. Your career is a remarkable example in innovation in engineering and in business. Talking about you also brought to mind my greatest regret.

I remember it well. While you were chancellor of the University of Waterloo and I was president, you said you wanted to devote some of your own money to create ten research chairs there. And you started to make good on that pledge, endowing chairs in architecture and in wireless communications.

The third chair you wished to fund was to study the subject of space in literature. Your reason was at once elegantly simple and far-reaching: science fiction enables us to ponder human existence in the universe and imagine how we might advance human life here on this planet and beyond in generations to come. This wish of yours convinced me you were not only a hard-headed engineer, but also a visionary romantic – a man who both thought and felt keenly.

Then you planned chairs in other fields with space as the common linking element. One was a chair in music about space, perhaps inspired by Gustav Holst's *The Planets*. Another was poetry inspired by space. I suggested one on the law of space. Together they totalled ten, for a start. You were trying do three things. First, cause us to expand our minds to a new and perhaps infinite frontier. Second, link disparate disciplines by offering a view through a common lens. Third, accentuate curiosity and excite the imagination. You might have invented the saying "Minds, like parachutes, work best when open."

Alas, you didn't live long enough to make your wish real, and I wasn't enterprising enough after your death to see your commitment through to completion. I regret my inability to do so. I'm sure universities in Canada have courses in their English curricula that enable students to study this genre of fiction, but you imagined a research chair that would bring together scholars, students, scientists, and entrepreneurs from a variety of disciplines – not just experts in literature – to delve deeply into space in literature and uncover insights we can translate into new ways of understanding ourselves, our world, and the universe, and maybe even actions we can take based on this revealed knowledge. You thought of today's fantasy as tomorrow's foundation.

Mike Lazaridis, our friend and your successor as chancellor at the University of Waterloo, was likely thinking along the same lines when he launched the Perimeter Institute for Theoretical Physics in 1999. He followed this with the Institute for Quantum Computing at the university, which he established because he believed that the classical laws of Newton, Einstein, and others do not explain what happens in very small spaces at the quantum level, and because he was passionate about our need to discover and learn. He knew his organizations would take years – even generations – to produce something truly remarkable, if anything at all. He considered the risk well worth taking. His decision was based on the very same combination of qualities you embodied: the hard-headed engineer and visionary romantic. Come to think of it, I should get in touch with Mike – there's this new research chair the two of us should talk about.

Your friend,
David

Michael Valentine (Val) O'Donovan (1939–2005) was born in Cork, Ireland. A gifted, award-winning engineer, he and his wife and their children immigrated to Canada in 1963 and settled in Montreal. After working in the satellite division of RCA Corporation for several years, he co-founded COM DEV, which under his direction soon became an international leader in the design and manufacture of space hardware. He capped his illustrious professional life serving as chancellor of the University of Waterloo from 1997 to 2003.

Stargazer, Earthgazer

Knowing our place in the world.

To Chris Hadfield

Dear Chris,

Whether kneeling in a canoe plunging headlong down a mighty river toward the unknown or floating weightlessly in space with only a slim tether to secure them from oblivion, those who explore new frontiers and reveal rare wonders share the same traits: intense curiosity, dogged determination, openness to collaborate, willingness to take calculated risks, expertise in the latest technologies, and a keen eye that doesn't merely observe but scrutinizes.

You displayed these characteristics throughout your career, most vividly as commander of the International Space Station. Your curiosity to investigate the unknown was piqued early when you watched the *Apollo 11* moon landing on television. Your determination is manifest in your long and prestigious career as a pilot and astronaut. Your skills as a collaborator were continually on display in the many roles you took on at the Canadian Space Agency and National Aeronautics and Space Administration. Your quick thinking was put to use on countless occasions during the days you were aboard the International Space Station and the nearly fifteen hours you spent spacewalking. And while orbiting the Earth, you took advantage of the most recent social media to connect with people and share your singular perspective to help those below gain a truer vision of their world and their place in it.

Your service aboard the International Space Station coincided almost perfectly with the 200th anniversary of the publication of the Map of the North-West Territory of the Province of Canada – also known as the Map of 1814. This remarkable document, which details the geography of millions of square kilometres of Canada stretching from Lake Superior to the Pacific Ocean, is the ultimate achievement of David Thompson. Another of our country's great explorers and discoverers, Thompson and his work show us that, while much in our lives has changed during the past two centuries, the tenets of exploration and discovery remain constant. Like you, Thompson was inquisitive and persistent. He was just sixteen years old when the Hudson's Bay Company first sent him to set up a trading post in the interior. Sixteen! To prepare for and carry out his heroic journeys, he gathered information from a wide range of sources – from First Peoples and fur traders, from oral accounts and written records. He embraced old and new technologies – canoe, compass, and sextant – to span great distances and to chart his travels, and all the while, he made painstakingly careful observations, measurements, and notes on his progress westward to the sea. The Salish-Flathead people of what is now British Columbia called him Koo Koo Sint, or Stargazer, because of his practice of navigating by the stars. Thompson looked far overhead – into the deepest visible recesses of space – to gain a truer sense of the land at his very feet and the course he must follow.

If he is Stargazer, you must be Earthgazer. You looked down from the vast expanse of space – hundreds of kilometres high – to give each of us below a truer sense of our place on Earth. You once said the thing people most wanted from space was a picture of their hometowns, and you concluded that this wish represented a universal ache to see how each of us fits in with everything around us. That sounds right to me. Your exploration and discovery satisfied an instinctual human yearning: we all want to understand where we are in relation to others, how each of us fits into the whole, and in which direction time and circumstance may be pushing us. You wrote tellingly about how gazing down at the surface of the planet as your spacecraft was in orbit granted you a special insight: we are all "crewmates on the same big ship, working and hoping for a little joy, some grace and better opportunities for our children." There is such wisdom in those words. Taking what you and Thompson have taught us, I would go a step further. You and Thompson show all people that the best way to grasp our true selves and our place in the world comes when we view ourselves from different perspectives. Thompson gazed up at the stars to comprehend his place and determine direction; you gazed down at the Earth to appreciate the commonality of our individual situations and our intrinsic relation to one another.

Yet we don't necessarily need to ride the rapids of a raging river or blast off in a rocket into space to gain perspectives different from our own. We can do so by reading, travelling, and listening to others. Not as adventurous perhaps, not as perilous either. We can read to increase the number of our perspectives. We can travel to intensify our perspectives. We can listen to others and use their experiences and observations to expand and enrich our perspectives. In these ways, each of us can be an explorer, a discoverer. Each of us can be a Stargazer or an Earthgazer.

A fellow gazer,
David

Chris Hadfield, an officer of the Order of Canada, is one of the most accomplished astronauts in the world. The top graduate of the U.S. Air Force Test Pilot School in 1988 and the U.S. Navy Test Pilot of the Year in 1991, he was selected by the Canadian Space Agency to be an astronaut in 1992. He was chief CapCom (the voice of mission control to astronauts in orbit) for twenty-five space shuttle launches and served as director of operations for NASA in Star City, Russia, from 2001 to 2003, chief of robotics for the NASA astronaut office in Houston from 2003 to 2006, and chief of International Space Station operations from 2006 to 2008. In March 2013, he became the first Canadian to assume command of the International Space Station. During his 146 days in space, he performed a record-setting number of experiments and oversaw an emergency spacewalk. He also used this voyage to share his passion for the arts and science with millions of people around the world via social media, gaining worldwide acclaim for his photographs from space and educational videos about life in space.

On June 27, 2013, Mr. Johnston awarded Commander Hadfield the Meritorious Service Cross (Civil Division), making him the first Canadian to hold both the civil and military decorations of this honour. In his post-astronaut career, Commander Hadfield is helping teach the Aviation Sciences program at the University of Waterloo, which was started in 2005 when Mr. Johnston was president of the school. The program is aimed at young people with an interest in aviation and space and, through co-op education, enables them to obtain their pilot's licence and a Bachelor of Sciences in Environmental Studies. It quickly became one of the university's most popular programs.

Constant Shield

Thoughts passing through Menin Gate.

To James Forrest Johnston and William Stonehouse

Dear Uncle Tot and Uncle William,

I can't begin to describe the horrors of war, thank God. Only those who have been in it can, and I'm not one. I never found myself in the muck and mire of the trenches; was never exposed to shrapnel and shell; never saw friends and comrades cut down beside me, then be forced to press on. Yet there are things I do understand: sadness and loss, service to country, and the onerous duty of the living to honour the dead.

What do I think of when I think of war? I think of the thousands upon thousands of Canadians who served in the First World War, Second World War, and Korean War, and in Afghanistan. Many never returned home. Those who did were forever transformed. I think too of those who were displaced and lost their homes, livelihoods, and the security we associate with peacetime. Such is the cost of war. Nations and governments; civilians and soldiers; men, women, and children – everyone feels the impact when war is waged; when guns, mortars, and tanks give voice to aggression, hostility, and hatred.

Our duty was vividly clear to me when I visited Menin Gate in Belgium this past year. I was humbled. Canadian divisions had passed along this spot in Flanders on the way to battle in the Great War. I tried to imagine the resolve and camaraderie of those soldiers. Did they march in silence, I wondered. Nervous conversation, perhaps? Could some foretell what was to come?

On the walls of the the Menin Gate Memorial to the Missing are 54,896 names of the British and Commonwealth soldiers lost in the Ypres Salient of the First World War – many of whom are Canadians. So young – mere lads mostly. The names are those of people without graves – those who went missing; those lost in the mud of Flanders; those whose ends we will never know. Each had a life waiting for him back home, a life curtailed and therefore unfulfilled. What promise, creativity, and ingenuity were lost with their deaths? Imagine what they might have achieved had they lived. I can't help wondering how would our world be different, be better. It staggers me to think that in a few short months 50,000 active human minds were simply taken off-line. It appeals to me therefore that to keep the memory of all those who have died serving our nation throughout our history, Canadians must strive to do better, work harder, build smarter and more caring communities, and make this a more just and fairer world. We must find a way to end conflicts for the sake of generations to come and for all those who fought and perished. We need only be brave enough to embrace peace. How wickedly elusive that obvious step seems to be.

When I was at Menin Gate, a young trumpeter sounded the Last Post. This call has echoed through those fields nearly 30,000 times since the end of the Great War. Every night at 8 p.m., the volunteer fire brigade gathers to honour the fallen who were never found. The strains of the trumpet are still poignant, reverent, riveting. As its last note faded, I thought of Canadians who have served alongside friends and allies throughout our history, and of those who continue to do so – with great conviction and real pride.

I thought of you, Uncle Tot. As a young man, you knew war. You fought with the First Canadian Army. You and your buddies liberated Holland in the forties – there's a note for a resumé. Sad to say, I don't know much more about your wartime experiences than that. While you lived a happy and long life, you would never talk about your war, even when pleaded with. Were your memories too agonizing? Could you not find words to do justice to your experiences? Or had you walled off that part of your life so solidly that you lost the ability to retrieve it? If so, I understand.

I thought of you too, Uncle William, though we never met. I was born in 1941 and you lived in the United States, where my mother grew up. You signed up and were part of a U.S. air bomber crew in Europe before I could meet you. Not long after, my grandparents received that fateful telegram stating that you and your crew had perished over Germany in the final months of the conflict. What sadness they must have felt. And what of you, your young life snuffed out in the anger of war? I have always regretted that we never got to know each other.

We Canadians are blessed to be a population long used to living in peace. And while we embrace reason as our guiding principle, we admit that, for some, hatred – and from it the urge to destroy – is a driving force. Knowing that, we still must ask the best among us to step forward, devote their lives to military training, and ready themselves on our behalf for the unexpected. Ultimately, we ask them to act swiftly in terrible times, risking injury and death so that others may stay safe. I'm astounded by the number and quality of Canadians who move to the front of the line to take on this role. The Canadian military – as it has been in times of peace and of conflict – is among the best-trained and most highly motivated forces in the world; no wonder that it is the most highly respected by Canadians of all our professions, callings, and trades. It remains our constant shield against villainy and enduring proof of the courage and goodness of human nature.

You were part of that shield. I promise that I shall never forget my duty to honour and remember the sacrifices made by you and by so many of your young friends.

With love,
David

Uncle Tot is James Forrest Johnston (1905–2001), who served in the Canadian Army in Europe in the Second World War. He is the younger brother of Mr. Johnston's father. A son, brother, husband, father, grandfather, great-grandfather, uncle, and friend, he died in 2001 at the age of ninety-six. Uncle William (1918–1945) was a younger brother of Mr. Johnston's mother. He was shot down and killed with his bomber crew on a sortie over Germany in 1945.

Love Made Visible

What service means to me.

To Walter Natynczyk

Dear Walt,

Service is love made visible. That kind of love is usually service to family, country, comrades, God, or humanity, whether these people are neighbours on your street or strangers on the other side of the world. Your career in the Canadian Army – dedicated to the service of our military and by extension to Canada – is a living example of that ethos.

You were kind enough to invite me to a gathering of your Army friends to mark your retirement from service in the Canadian Armed Forces. I'll always remember what you said at the mess hall party, because it perfectly sums up the idea of service as love made visible. You told us that the biggest change in your professional life came when you were promoted to lieutenant colonel at an unusually young age. You were thrilled, because while you knew from the time you were a teenager that you wanted a career in the military, you never believed you could achieve such a rank, let alone reach it so soon. That elation lasted for twenty-four hours. Then, you told us, you realized in a moment of profound insight you must shift your focus. You no longer thought of your great personal achievement but about how you were going to serve the regiment you were assigned to lead. A great burden came off your shoulders when you became aware you were no longer going to centre your career on advancing yourself but on serving others. You moved from first-person singular to first-person plural – from me to we in your centre of gravity. You revealed that awareness of service beyond self for the rest of your career. It's why I've told you that, if I had one wish in life, it would be that we had a farm next to yours so that whenever my grandchildren were there I could send them over the fence to help you cut wood or mow the grass – for some of your values, especially that of service, surely would rub off on them.

Your career is also a credit to the Canadian Armed Forces. Through your example, our armed forces as an institution showed all its personnel that service to comrades and to country is a springboard to further advancement, not an impediment to it. I witnessed this celebration of service time and again as governor general at military events and functions across Canada and around the world – never more clearly than at ceremonies to repatriate troops from service in Afghanistan. I know those ceremonies – and their honour of service – meant a great deal to you, too. Canada's men and women in uniform didn't call you Uncle Walt for nothing. These men and women served with courage, sacrificed their lives, endured the extremes both of climate and of separation, and through it all proved their diligence, toughness, and compassion for the plight of others. When the last of the troops returned home on March 18, 2014, I was privileged to be at CFB Trenton to greet them. That homecoming marked the end of more than a dozen years of our Canadian mission in Afghanistan – a mission with a certain aim, yet in an operational theatre that threw everything it had at our men and women in uniform. Afghanistan tested their heads, hearts, and guts. Our soldiers dug deep, putting all their training into practice and learning new tactical skills on the move – skills that will form the training of the generation of soldiers who are readying themselves now to meet the high standards that these veterans have set. They also bore witness to the suffering of a population under the tyranny of deliberate violence, enforced poverty, and perverse fanaticism. They saw the worst and the best of humanity, and while many of them brought home images that will haunt them, they carry also the memories of encounters that will inspire them for the rest of their lives.

Over the course of the Afghanistan mission, our men and women in uniform undertook many roles: as soldiers of course, but also as ambassadors, as peacekeepers, as protectors and rebuilders of civil society, and as teachers to Afghanistan's own security force. Many talents, many roles: that versatility is a Canadian legacy and, I believe, one of the greatest assets our country had on the ground. The selfless service of those in the mission markedly improved the fortunes and futures of the Afghan people, whose dignity, opportunity, and very rights our men and women travelled so far to uphold. Through it all, these men and women put themselves at ultimate risk – 158 of them perished – standing their ground in defence of our beliefs and getting the job done so that those they came to help got that help. Their service is a love of country, comrades, and humanity made visible.

At the end of my first visit to Afghanistan, the senior U.S. military officer serving as liaison with our Canadian troops said to me, "I have two profound observations about Canadians in action. As professional soldiers they are second to none in the world, but they also have the ability to take off the armour and operate as civilian leaders – bringing order out of chaos, rebuilding schools and hospitals, reorganizing a destroyed village into a functioning community with an effective local government. I never thought I would see this from soldiers in a military theatre. For a long time I thought it was your unique training. But I've come to believe it is the voluntary notion of the Canadian military; those who choose to serve reflect the best of fundamental Canadian values."

Joanna Baillie, a Scottish poet, nearly two centuries ago wrote, "Service is the rent we pay for our space on this earth." Her statement remains just as true today. In its spirit, I'm safe in saying your bill and that of the men and women of Canada's Afghanistan mission can be stamped "Paid in full."

Thank you for your service,
David

Walter Natynczyk is deputy minister of Veterans Affairs Canada. He joined the Canadian Forces in 1975, beginning a professional life that saw him assume a variety of roles and took him around the world – most notably as a peacekeeper in Cyprus, Croatia, and Bosnia and Herzegovina; commander of the Royal Canadian Dragoons; and deputy commanding general with U.S. III Corps in Iraq while a military exchange officer. He capped his thirty-seven-year career in the Canadian military when he was appointed Chief of the Defence Staff in 2008, serving in the post until 2012. He retired from the Canadian Army with the rank of general. He became president of the Canadian Space Agency before being appointed deputy minister of Veterans Affairs Canada. His life of service continues.

To Make and to Unmake

Saluting John McCrae.

To Michael McKay

Dear Michael,

Thank you for inviting me to take part in the ceremony to unveil the statue of John McCrae in Guelph. The event generated in me a feeling of bittersweet pleasure.

The pleasure, I think, is obvious. The unveiling commemorates a singular person and achievement in our country's history – Lieutenant Colonel McCrae and his iconic poem "In Flanders Fields." What is especially touching is that the ceremony took place almost exactly one hundred years to the day on which McCrae wrote his verse. It's remarkable that a poem written near the front lines on a scrap of paper should have survived the First World War when its author and many millions of others didn't. Remarkable, too, that John McCrae should be remembered all these years later for a single fifteen-line rondeau rather than for his skills as a doctor.

He was an exceptional physician, as you know. Yet it's not widely understood that prior to the war McCrae interned with Dr. William Osler, the renowned Canadian who has been called the father of modern medicine. In fact, Dr. John Adami of McGill University, McCrae's teacher and mentor, called McCrae the most talented physician of his generation. I marvel at that fact. The most talented physician of his generation!

This detail brings me to the bittersweet. Much as I love "In Flanders Fields" for its poignant message of remembrance, I lament McCrae had occasion to write it. Just imagine what he might have achieved were he to have lived in a time of peace. Think of him as a family doctor or specialist practising in his hometown, or advancing medical knowledge and practice in one of our country's great teaching hospitals, rather than dealing with pointless carnage and untold suffering in a muddy trench or aid station near Ypres. Just imagine what he could have accomplished in the medical field in peacetime were he not serving in the desolate fields of Flanders.

Alas, what could have been was not to be. And while the poppy is a worldwide symbol of remembrance thanks to Lieutenant Colonel McCrae's verse, John McCrae himself is symbolic of something else entirely: the terrible waste of human life and potential that was the First World War. The most talented physician of his generation dead of pneumonia before war's ended, exhausted, aged forty-five. Such a crime.

Some might think McCrae's desire to write poetry in the midst of a global cataclysm to be a hopeless, futile act. But I think it's an entirely understandable response to the horrors of war. The word "poem" itself is derived from the Greek word for "to make." If a poem is "a thing made," the First World War was surely its opposite. It unmade. Human lives and families, cities and towns, whole countries and an entire civilization brought to ruin. One of our duties in remembering those who served is to remember that war is never glorious – not even when rendered into verse. War means we've failed to resolve our differences by other means. And when we fail, real people pay a terrible price. Real people such as John McCrae.

I don't know if I told you or not at the unveiling ceremony but I had the privilege of visiting the site in Belgium where John McCrae served and is presumed to have written "In Flanders Fields." While there, I imagined what went through his mind as he scribbled down those fifteen lines in the space of a few minutes – the sadness, the defiance, the desire to create something of lasting worth when all of value about him was being ripped apart. That may be his greatest legacy and one we preserve with the memorial you and your group worked so hard to bring into being – the Canadian impulse to make when all about is being unmade.

Thank you,
David

Honorary Colonel Michael McKay is chairman of the McCrae Statue Project Committee. The committee organized the effort to have a statue of Lieutenant Colonel John McCrae constructed and erected in Guelph, Ontario, McCrae's hometown. The Royal Regiment of Canadian Artillery commissioned sculptor Ruth Abernethy to create the statue, which depicts McCrae at the historic moment he completed the poem for which he is famous.

Part Two

What Consumes Me

Stand Up, Speak Up, Sit Down

Advice to my successors about speechmaking.

To my successors

Dear governors general of the future,

I have delivered 250 or so speeches each year during my time as governor general – everything from impromptu remarks before informal gatherings to lengthy orations to members of Parliament and senators assembled to mark the opening of a new session of Parliament. I have gained from this experience what one might term a *discordant relationship* with speeches; they are the most inefficient way to communicate widely because each speech is a singular event that takes place at a specific time and place, yet this very inefficiency heightens the potential influence of speeches on those who carve out the time to attend them. These people get to look at you (sometimes right in the eye), hear your voice, and see the expressions on your face and movements of your body. For flesh-and-blood audiences, then, speeches can still say a lot – even in a day when the directly spoken word is eclipsed by so many other media.

Each of you will no doubt make many hundreds of speeches of your own during your tenures in this office. With this fact in mind, allow me to pass along a very brief counsel about speech-making. It comes from my grandmother. She told me that on any and all occasions at which I'm called on to speak, I should stand up to be seen, speak up to be heard, and sit down to be appreciated. The third element of her directive is often the most important for us speechmakers – for when we neglect to follow the first of these two commands, our audiences certainly want us to follow the third. In the spirit of my grandmother's sage advice, I'll now sit down, so to speak.

Yours in brevity,
David

P.S. As W.C. Fields once observed: "There are smiles *wherever* I go. There are more smiles *whenever* I go."

As of writing, there have been twenty-eight governors general of Canada. Although this office dates to 1867, it can be argued that the institution of the Crown's representative on this land dates to 1627 with the appointment of Samuel de Champlain as the first governor of New France. One wonders how many speeches he gave.

Reclaiming the Game

Rid hockey of fighting.

To Ralph "Cooney" Weiland

Dear Cooney,

The most Canadian moment of my time as governor general took place not in Canada but on the other side of the world. I was with my wife, Sharon, in New Delhi, India, at the High Commissioner's residence while we were on a state visit. With others there, we were watching a special event: Canada was playing the United States for the men's Olympic hockey championship. When the Canadian team won in a thrilling game, everyone stood to sing "O Canada" to celebrate. We all did. It was the loudest, proudest, heartiest rendition of our national anthem that I've ever been a part of.

That the game we love to play and watch and cheer was at the centre of one of my most cherished memories comes as no surprise to me. Hockey is a product of our country. It evolved out of the very physical nature of Canada – of our winters that last from the start of November to the middle of April; of the countless frozen rivers, streams, and ponds that pattern our land; of the tens of thousands of small-town rinks in which men, women, and children gather morning, noon, and night. The game is also, I think, a reflection of who we are as a people. We're hardy and hard working. We do the tough tasks it takes to succeed. We shun the limelight. We prefer being a good teammate, knowing we can accomplish more together than we can on our own. We're a nation of grinders, not floaters or cherry pickers.

And yet our game is not static. It has changed as we have changed. The happiest change is the involvement of women and girls. As women in our country have struggled to gain the equality of opportunity that is their right, they have found a sporting home in the game. In fact, in the Sochi Winter Olympics, our women won the hockey gold medal against the United States in sudden-death overtime. The most exciting and best-contested athletic competitions I have watched for the past two decades have been between the Canadian and U.S. women's hockey teams. Women and girls are taking up hockey in increasing numbers not only in Canada but also throughout North America and around the world. And the qualities that we love about the men's game are also on display when women play – speed, skill, playmaking, teamwork.

I'm a big fan of women playing hockey. While I served as honorary patron of the 2013 women's world championship, when the tournament was held in Ottawa, my connection lies even closer to home. As you know, my wife and I have five daughters. Our eldest plays in a women's league in her hometown. Our numbers one and two daughters played intramural hockey at McGill for the law team. Our third daughter followed me to Harvard – our alma mater – and played on the women's team, and then to Cambridge where she captained and coached the women's ice hockey squad. Our numbers four and five daughters both play pickup hockey. Our daughters represent many thousands of women and girls across Canada who have achieved a great deal in our game in a very short period of time. Many young women – Justine Blainey comes immediately to mind – had to battle to play organized hockey because of the close-minded thinking of many men in the game. All Canadians – not just those who love hockey – owe these courageous, pioneering women a debt of gratitude.

On the flip side, Canadian girls can now benefit from the valuable lessons that the game teaches. I learned many of these lessons from the game and from you specifically. You taught me to concentrate on doing, not merely saying, and to focus on doing the things I could control. You taught me to have no regrets about the decisions I've made, to never look back, to get on with the task at hand. You taught me the value of the team's maximizing the strengths of individuals and minimizing their weaknesses without at any time the matter becoming about the person in question. You taught me that success is nearly always the result of a group's effort to reduce mistakes to the smallest possible degree and not due to individual heroics. This thinking reflected your scorn for the glorification of the hero and the excessive attention paid to the celebration of the individual in modern life. To you, life, like hockey, is a team game. We win together; I fail when I choose to go it alone.

The lessons I learned from you on the ice have been remarkably wise steering influences for me in how I've handled life's difficulties and demands as a husband, father, lawyer, teacher, and executive. That doesn't mean my playing days are over. I still lace up my skates, grab a stick, and put on a helmet regularly during the winter months at what I call the oldest rink in North America. It's an almost-full-size rink just outside Rideau Hall. It was on this rink that Arthur and Algernon – two sons of Lord Stanley of Preston – played for the Ottawa Rideau Hall Rebels more than a century ago and inspired their father to sponsor a cup to recognize the best team in the land. A cup that, one day, would have your name etched on it. A few times!

My activity in the game has extended off the ice. I've used my time as governor general to call on the National Hockey League and amateur leagues across Canada to bring an effective end to all headshots and fighting in the game. Headshots should be gone and fighting should be gone. Hockey is the greatest game in the world. And it is so because it is faster than anything else. That speed – combined with the playmaking, the intensity, the intricacies, the virtuosity, along with the consciousness of five good teammates on the ice with you at any one time – make it just a beautiful game. And those are the qualities we want to emphasize. Not the taking off of the gloves and beating up one another, or using a stick or a heavily armoured elbow on an opponent's head or face, or crushing an opponent into the boards from the blind side.

The time for debating over whether head injuries, however inflicted, are dangerous to health is no longer useful. Scientific evidence is growing that repeated concussions – and even multiple sub-concussive brain injuries – are linked to a condition called chronic traumatic encephalopathy, an irreversible ailment that progressively destroys brain tissue and leads to dementia. We're starting to see more of the consequences of fighting and headshots. Derek Boogaard, a designated fighter from junior through to the pro ranks, died at twenty-eight from an accidental drug and alcohol overdose while recovering from a concussion. A posthumous examination of his brain found he had suffered damage more advanced than that seen in some former enforcers who had died in middle age. The fact that players are much bigger and faster than ever before, combined with fighting, means that an increasing number of players are suffering injuries – some clear, some hidden – that will haunt them for the rest of their lives. Hockey analytics – drawing conclusions about how the game is played and the performance of specific players by gathering and examining huge amounts of data – tells us that the number of fighters and fights in the professional game is dropping and will continue to drop based on the limited utility of these kinds of players. That said, I believe we will need much more vigorous leadership and not just statistically based trends to regain the best of the game and ban the unnecessary violence.

Yet professional hockey is not my single focus. I stress the pro game because in many ways it sets the tone for how the game is played elsewhere in our country. I'm concerned about hockey played at all levels, by all ages, by boys and girls, men and women, and I'm concerned about what our acceptance of fighting and headshots says to all those who play the game. Hockey is our national sport, because we've always thought of it as embodying qualities that we possess and hold dear: toughness, tenacity, and teamwork. How can we square these virtues with fighting and goon tactics? We can't. It's impossible. We can't equate ourselves with only the best attributes of the game and divorce ourselves from its ugly side. Looking at the matter from another perspective, our whole history as a country has been one of avoiding conflict and usually finding consensus and compromise. Does that attitude translate to sports? I think it does. We Canadians are known as people who are tenacious and competitive, but we're also known as a highly civilized people in how we conduct ourselves. And when I see on TV the amount of fighting going on and the goonery, they are not qualities we want to celebrate in our game. Those are not the qualities we Canadians want to teach our boys and girls. I want my grandchildren to be able to play hockey, and to be able to play the game at its greatest speed and at its most competitive, but to do so in a way that is civilized and doesn't encourage a kind of thuggery.

As you know, I speak from some experience. I suffered three concussions the year I turned sixteen – two from football, one from hockey. After I'd been feeling dizzy and sick for days, our family doctor cleared me to return to the ice on the condition that I start wearing a helmet. No other players did at the time. But the command was wear a helmet or don't play. Pretty easy decision for me. We both also know one can play hard-nosed hockey without fighting. When we played, we were both small guys surviving and thriving in a tough game. I'm a few inches under six feet tall, and back when I was on the Crimson blue line I weighed 150 pounds. (I weigh just a little more than that now.) I got my share of penalties for playing tenaciously in the corners and in front of the net, but I don't recall ever being in a fight. Now I'm not going to argue the game in our respective eras wasn't rough at times and that we didn't play with and against some nasty guys. You taught me to play tough, just to come out of the corner with the puck and my teeth. Eddie Shore – one of the toughest defencemen the game has ever seen – was your teammate for years. He stood at less than six feet tall and weighed about 190 pounds. A big man in his day, he would be one of the smaller players in today's game. Now the average National Hockey League defenceman is six feet two inches tall and weighs 210 pounds – bigger than most I played with or against. That's a lot of bulk to put behind a shoulder, elbow, or fist.

Can we eliminate fighting and headshots from the game at all levels? My answer is this: Of course! What's stopping us? We make changes all the time to improve our quality of life.

We recycle waste, we wear seatbelts in our cars, we no longer smoke in such great numbers. We're smart people. We change what we do when we have clear evidence that our behaviours are hurting us. Provinces and municipalities across Canada have banned people from smoking in bars and restaurants. Owners of these places said these new laws would sound the death knell for their operations. Things did change. Turns out bars and restaurants are more popular than ever, and fewer people are suffering heart attacks and lung diseases as a result of second-hand smoke.

So what should we do? I want headshots to be a thing of the past. We can start by making equipment that protects those who wear it and doesn't injure other players. We can also continue making the penalties for blows to the head more severe. The NHL and the three main junior leagues in Canada have increased penalties and suspensions for headshots recently. The junior leagues have even stepped up penalties for unintentional blows to the head. But far too many headshots are delivered and suffered by players in those leagues and elsewhere. And much of the good that stiffer penalties deliver is mitigated by the fact that these leagues sanction and even encourage fighting. How can league officials have a more severe penalty for, say, a single unintentional elbow to the head (a five-minute major and an immediate game misconduct) than a fight (a two-minute minor or five-minute major) that results in two players inflicting and suffering multiple intentional blows to the head? Makes no sense to me.

I also want fighting to be a thing of the past. Fighting should result in an instant game misconduct; a second fight would be a five-game suspension. In any other North American team sport – football, baseball, basketball – they deal with fighting with this kind of severity. It's not excused as a safety valve for players to blow off a head of steam. Not that you would ever, ever lose your cool, Cooney. As for the argument that if you eliminate fighting you will force players to retaliate with stick work, you deal with that type of retaliation with equally harsh penalties. Other sports manage to do it and don't seem to have those consequences. That's why I want to see more severe penalties for slashing, which I see as a deliberate attempt to lift up your stick and use it like a club. Some people argue that two players fighting do so consensually and therefore they should be permitted to fight. Just because two players want to do something on the ice, does that make it right? Does that make it acceptable? And to those who say fighting is an exciting and therefore indispensable part of the game, I would respond by asking a few more questions. How many fights do we see during the Stanley Cup playoffs or during the Memorial Cup tournament? Very few, if any. How many fights do we see during the Olympics or World Cup? None that I can recall. In these tournaments, are the players any less determined to win? Are the games any less exciting? Are fans any less passionate about what they're watching? No, no, and no! I should be careful: my words are getting awfully close to a pep talk, and we both know you didn't believe in them.

To make real the solutions I suggest and others, we would all do well to apply a few of your lessons. We should concentrate on doing, not merely saying. The scientific proof is compelling and grows more persuasive every day. Fighting and headshots are producing career-ending injuries and life-diminishing ailments among players. What's more, as players grow bigger and stronger, as the game becomes faster and these larger players hit with increasing force, we can expect an ever-expanding number and percentage of players to suffer these injuries and ailments, if all other factors remain the same. The time for talking is over. We need to act and we need to act now.

We should focus on doing the things we can control. We'll never be able to outlaw all headshots, no matter how onerous the penalties we impose. The speed and physical nature of the game make some collisions unavoidable – including those that result in blows to the head. But that reality shouldn't prevent us from taking action to reduce their number so they become extraordinarily rare occurrences and not regular ones.

We should draw on the strengths of others. We can learn what leagues, officials, physicians, and scientists across Canada and around the world are doing to make the game less violent and reduce the number of injuries caused by headshots. These solutions might be new penalties or new parameters for existing infractions. They might be better kinds of equipment. They might be improved training for coaches and referees. They might be targeted teaching to show players the proper way to initiate contact and to make them more aware of the consequences of fighting and headshots.

We should work together, each making the most of our distinctive strengths. We can take the best methods we learn, share them freely, and look to our leaders in the game to follow up and make sure the best methods are implemented as widely as possible. And we should focus much energy on the young – those who are just learning the game.

Cooney, you never fooled me. I always knew you were much smarter than you let on to your Harvard players, especially when you would start a sentence by saying, "I've got only a Grade 10 education. . . ." That's why I know we can apply your lessons from decades in hockey to rid the game of fighting and headshots. What an incredible and important legacy for this generation of Canadians to leave future generations in our country and the game we love.

Go Crimson!
David

Ralph "Cooney" Weiland (1904–1985) enjoyed an illustrious career in hockey, both on the ice and behind the bench. A native of Seaforth, Ontario, he was a member of the Owen Sound Greys team that won the Memorial Cup in 1924 as the top junior squad in Canada. He went on to play eleven seasons in the National Hockey League, capturing the scoring title in 1930 and winning the Stanley Cup with the Boston Bruins in 1928–29 and 1938–39 – the second time as the team's captain. Following his playing days, Cooney Weiland coached the Bruins to a Cup victory in 1940–41; piloted teams in the

American Hockey League for six seasons; and led Harvard University's men's varsity hockey team from 1950 to 1971. (Mr. Johnston was a Crimson defenceman for four of these years – 1959 to 1963 – and a first-team All American for two. He was also named to the top fifty hockey players in the last half-century in the U.S. Eastern Collegiate Athletic Conference and is an inductee to the Harvard Athletic Hall of Fame.) Upon his retirement from the game, Cooney Weiland received two of hockey's highest honours: he was inducted into the Hockey Hall of Fame in 1971 and was given the Lester Patrick Award the following year to recognize his contribution to the game in the United States.

An Individual Institution

The essential function of our governor general.

To Jacques Monet

Dear Jacques,

This letter is overdue. I have long admired your ongoing efforts to help Canadians understand the role of the representatives of the Crown in Canada. Yours has been a valuable undertaking, for the position of governor general in our country is one shrouded in mystery and misunderstanding. As you know, the governor general is not Canada's head of state. That designation remains with our Sovereign. Nor is the office one that can have a meaningful, direct influence on government legislation and policy. And yet neither is it wholly ceremonial – "a post," as one columnist put it, "occupied by a tea-and-crumpets do-gooder, all sugar and smile."

So what is it? I consider it an institution and an individual.

As an institution, the governor general represents our country's head of state – in our case, the Queen of Canada. The primary function of the governor general is to uphold Canada's system of responsible government. Constitutional expert Eugene Forsey defines responsible government as government by a Cabinet answerable to and removable by a majority of the elected assembly, which in our country's case is the House of Commons. An impartial and apolitical head of state is essential to our system of responsible government. Peter Hogg, another of our leading constitutional scholars, summed up this point nicely: a system of responsible government cannot work without a formal head of state who is possessed of certain reserve powers. With no Crown and no governor general to represent that institution, there would be no responsible government in Canada as we know it. I find the metaphor used by political scientist Frank McKinnon to be particularly vivid and instructive. He likens the office of the governor general to a constitutional fire extinguisher – a potent mixture of powers for use in great urgencies. Like fire extinguishers, Professor McKinnon notes, these emergency powers appear in bright colours and are strategically located. And while everyone hopes they will never be used, the fact that they are not does not render them useless.

These words could not be truer. The occasions on which the governor general must exercise the reserve powers of the Crown are exceedingly rare, but these powers are of supreme importance to ensure that Canada always has a government in place – one with the confidence of the House of Commons and, therefore, safeguarding the rights and freedoms of Canadians – constitutional values that flow unbroken across some eight hundred years from the Magna Carta. As the Department of Canadian Heritage publication *A Crown of Maples* states, power is entrusted to governments to use only temporarily on behalf of the people, so long as Parliament continues to show confidence in their actions. In our country, the government rules while the Crown reigns. Indeed, the office of the governor general shows us how much institutions matter in preserving peaceful, orderly societies. Her Majesty Queen Elizabeth II stated that one of the strongest and most valued aspects of this particular institution is the stability and continuity that it can bring from the past into the present – a truth that is particularly valuable in a country as geographically vast and culturally diverse as Canada. Without healthy, vigorous national institutions, we might be forgiven for asking, "What is Canada?"

Individuals matter, too – especially in the office of the governor general. This post is not an abstract model to be contemplated in theory alone. Nor is it a simple mechanism that is turned on at specific times to generate predetermined actions. Like our Sovereign herself – who has served Canada so well and who has for so long expressed the values of service, steadfastness, and tolerance that we all hold as Canadian ideals – the office is occupied by a living, breathing person. My predecessors contributed a great deal to the development of this office and thus to the progress of Canada. I can think of few national institutions from which individuals have exerted such a profound influence, and the story of each viceregal mandate is fascinating, instructive, and relevant to its times. I resist singling any one of them out, for each made a special contribution in his or her way. Each was reflective of a unique background and set of experiences, and each brought to the job a particular love for Canada and concerns for the well-being of Canadians. Knowing that each governor general is an individual – a human being with a family, previous career, personal story, and special way of seeing this country and the world – enables Canadians to connect with this vital element of their government on a personal level removed from the divisiveness and often rancour of political affiliation and partisanship.

This blend of the individual and the institutional makes the office of the governor general both deeply personal and decidedly practical. I cannot think of any words that better capture this blend and its value to our country than your own: "The Crown shows us that our democratic inheritance descends to us through real people, each with a role to play in preserving our institutions and expressing ourselves. The repeated, measured flow of ritual reminds us that the Canadian Crown and who represent it – the Queen, the Governor General and Lieutenant Governors – are symbols of our freedom and ideals."

Thank you, Jacques, for shining such a brilliant light on this individual institution.

David

Jacques Monet is one of the foremost experts on the Crown in Canada and the role of our country's governor general. An ordained priest, Father Monet served as advisor to Governor General Jules Léger from 1974 to 1979 and is author of *The Canadian Crown*, published in 1979.

Grampa Book

The power of reading and writing.

To Miss Wilkinson

Dear Miss Wilkinson,

I've been called plenty of names during the many, many years that have passed since I was in your grade 10 English class at Sault Collegiate Institute. My favourite by far is Grampa Book. It's what my grandchildren call me. Yes, young Davey Johnston has grandchildren. Twelve of them, an even dozen! They're fascinating kids. They call me Grampa Book because I'm seldom seen without a book in my hands – often more than one. I'm constantly sharing books, stories, and quotations. And I take every opportunity I get to read to my grandchildren, introducing them to worlds they have never seen before, and through them and this experience, I revisit old worlds with fresh eyes. I try to tell them stories they have never heard before. But of course I have stories I'm particularly fond of retelling – like *The Chronicles of Narnia* by C.S. Lewis. I'm rereading it to my grandchildren, having already shared the series of books five times with my five daughters.

Encountering new ideas and gaining greater context of ones I've encountered already are the main pleasures of reading. I can't think of an experience any more intellectually and emotionally pleasing and transformative. I can, however, get impatient with books. If one doesn't seize my attention and propel me on in the first twenty pages or so, I don't hesitate to cast it aside. And when I pick up a work of non-fiction, I often scrutinize the table of contents and the book's final pages to determine whether I want to devote my time and attention to the whole thing. Drives my wife crazy. And some books I return to after many years for a second read. In fact, I'm now working through Will and Ariel Durant's *History of Civilization* series for a third time.

You introduced me to the power of words. You first showed me how reading pretty much anything but especially great literature serves as a lens through which we can view our lives and our changing world. What a gift you shared with me. I like how novelist E.L. Doctorow expressed the electric force of reading. He said any book you pick up as a reader is a private circuit for your own life to flow through. In that way, the act of reading is a powerful source of good in the world. I believe that as people become more cosmopolitan – as they become familiar with the experiences of people from many different countries and cultures – the harder it becomes for them to dehumanize others. Reading breeds empathy.

This thought is not especially novel – ahem. Steven Pinker wrote that fiction especially is empathy technology. In his book *The Better Angels of Our Nature*, the Harvard University professor made a case for the invention of printing and the subsequent "Republic of Letters" of the seventeenth and eighteenth centuries spreading ideas that led to a humanitarian revolution. He argued convincingly that some popular novels in the nineteenth century, such as *Oliver Twist* and *Uncle Tom's Cabin*, propelled that revolution further by encouraging readers to put themselves in the place of people much different from themselves. When we step into the shoes of others – even just for a few moments – we enrich our own lives and expand the scope of our moral concern. Of course, the empathy that books ignite in us is not inexhaustible. But books and reading can be a darn good way to nurture greater empathy in all of us, especially in young people.

The flip side to reading, of course, is writing. Writing requires you to crystallize your thoughts. I never know what I truly think until I sit down at a keyboard or pick up a pen and try to express it in words. It's tough work, but there are few feelings more gratifying than the one you get when you capture on the page an idea or emotion you think is worth sharing. Nothing good ever comes without a struggle. I learned this lesson clearly when I was dean of the law faculty at

Western University in the 1970s. Very few of our faculty members then had their work published in scholarly journals. Even fewer were writing books despite the fact that there was a hunger for volumes on Canadian jurisprudence in a multitude of fields. I thought it important to lead and so produced several books of my own. We also brought publishers' representatives to the faculty twice a year to encourage our younger professors to write books. We quickly boosted the number of books produced by our professors from one a year to eight or ten. Each year, we would have a baptismal ceremony in which we would unveil publicly for all the university to see the books written by our faculty members. It was a celebration of writing. Then we displayed them permanently in a case at the entrance of our library to remind our students of the importance of books and the valuable role of their professors in writing them and continually reforming the law.

Writing is something worth celebrating. Where would readers be without writers? Some of the most memorable evenings I spend as governor general are those on which I meet writers, translators, and illustrators at ceremonies to honour winners of the Governor General's Literary Awards. John Buchan started the awards. Also known as Lord Tweedsmuir, he served as governor general from 1935 to 1940. He was a prolific Scot who produced more than 120 books during his lifetime. My favourite room at Rideau Hall is the library, which contains every Governor General's Literary Award–winning book since 1936 and has Buchan's portrait hanging over the fireplace. I wish it had been possible for you to attend one of the awards ceremonies. You would have relished meeting the writers. They help define our country's identity for Canadians and spread aspects of our shared identity with readers not only across Canada but also throughout the world. Robertson Davies, one of our great writers (and a Governor General's Literary Awards winner), wrote that a nation without a literature is not a nation. I would add that a nation that ignores its literature and languages, that neglects to teach and encourage children to read and write, is not a nation either; or if it is a nation, it is one without a soul and an inspiration.

I can't imagine what my life would have held without reading and writing. And I can't think of reading and writing without thinking of you and your influence. For that, for you, I am and will be eternally grateful.

Your devoted student,
David

Miss Wilkinson was Mr. Johnston's grade 10 English teacher at Sault Collegiate Institute in Sault Ste. Marie, Ontario. Her inspiration and tutelage helped him win the school's prize for poetry in grade 10 and the prize for prose the next year. Miss Wilkinson's influence has been lasting: Mr. Johnston has written twenty-seven books, primarily legal treatises, including new editions and co-authored works. The books are mainly co-authored because Mr. Johnston worked in teams with former students. One was co-authored with his daughter Debbie, a lawyer with the Department of Justice. Sharon Johnston, who was also taught by Miss Wilkinson, has done her share as well, publishing scientific articles and her first novel, based on her grandmother's life. She is working on a second, based on her mother's life in Sault Ste. Marie; a third is also planned, which Mrs. Johnston will entitle *The Boy in the Orange Pyjamas*. Mr. Johnston hopes he's "the boy."

How Smart and Caring Are We?

Happiness is something we can measure.

To John F. Helliwell

Dear John,

What gets measured gets done. I'm sure you of all people are familiar with Peter Drucker's famous axiom. If only it were entirely true! My long experience – in higher education especially – shows me that many things we do aren't a consequence of our measuring them, and many things we measure with the intention of doing them don't get done. Put another way, not everything that is counted counts, and not everything that counts can be counted. That said, I believe Drucker's phrase often applies when it comes to building the smart and caring Canada we all desire. Smart and caring is the highest characterization to which any country can aspire. In my installation address entitled "A Smart and Caring Country: A Call to Service," I described a smart and caring country as one that supports families and children, reinforces learning and innovation, and encourages philanthropy and volunteerism – laudable goals.

Yet how do we communicate the value of these goals and chart our progress toward them? Just how smart and caring are we? We must measure. Despite my qualifications of Drucker's phrase, it's the only practical way to keep us focused and engaged in the quest. Keenness of mind and kindness of heart are not abstract, ephemeral qualities floating about in the morning mist. They are national traits to which we can assign value and can track over time. I know you agree. Your work to measure individual and mass happiness has been groundbreaking, especially your effort to produce the *World Happiness Report*. It has informed and inspired my thinking about how to make our country smarter and more caring.

Three main points you make through the report stand out to me. The first is how much our happiness is tied to our trust in public institutions. We are happier when we believe these institutions behave honestly, honourably, and in our interests and not in the interests of the people who happen to occupy positions of authority. People in many countries throughout the world lack this trust in their public institutions – for good reason. All these people want – all any of us wants – is a fair shot at achieving meaningful, fulfilling lives. We want our public institutions, in which we invest so many resources and even more faith, to serve us as we strive to enjoy those lives.

The second insight I gained from your work is just how vital it is to invest in the early development of children. When we raise happy kids, we not only give them a great and deserving gift, but we also equip them to grow up and become adults who can contribute mightily to the overall social and economic well-being of our country. In doing so, we create a virtuous cycle of happiness that perpetuates itself and grows stronger over time.

A finding that stood out to me is how much more happiness we derive from the wealth of our social connections than from the wealth of our bank accounts. Money gives us a baseline of security and freedom, but it is the number and quality of our human relationships – and the generosity of thought and action that flows from these relationships – that bring true richness to our lives. One of the most important factors in making these connections is empathy. The older I get and the more I experience, the more I consider empathy to be the most important quality we can exhibit as adults and teach our young people. Now I don't mean the strict definition of empathy as feeling someone else's pain. That sentiment alone can be unhelpful and even destructive. Empathy is taking the time to fully understand the circumstances and motivations of people and not rushing to judgement based on biases or stereotypes. Which skill could be more influential to the success of our entire country than that our citizens have the ability to understand the feelings and condition of their fellows?

Gaining that understanding and then acting on it in a targeted way is why we measure happiness, isn't it? When I refer to happiness, I don't mean anything abstract. The United States

Declaration of Independence refers to the inalienable right of all people to pursue happiness. The pursuit of happiness in that context is the freedom to achieve personal fulfillment however each person defines it. Happiness today is gauged differently and more literally – not only personal freedom, but also income level, healthy years of life expectancy, availability of social support, personal and collective generosity, and freedom from corruption in government and business. In using these measures, you and your colleagues who produced the *World Happiness Report* have broadened the scope by which government can assess the state of their citizens' well-being. Your work is also important in prompting statistical agencies within individual countries to start collecting the kind of data they require to measure happiness and apply some of the lessons learned from the happiest countries.

I see your pioneering work in measuring individual and collective happiness reflected in the Canadian Index of Wellbeing. The brainchild of the Atkinson Charitable Foundation and now housed at the University of Waterloo Faculty of Applied Health Sciences, the index delves into eight key measures that I believe are fundamental to understanding and producing a smarter, more caring country, especially in the Canadian context: the vitality of our communities and of our leisure and cultural activities; the quality of our education, our environment, and our living standards; the health of our different populations; our engagement in our democratic way of life; and the ways we choose to put our time to use.

These indicators measure what truly matters to Canadians: Do we care about the physical and mental health of our neighbours and fellow citizens? Do all men and women have opportunities to prosper? Are we engaged in the public lives of our communities and country? Do we have sufficient time outside of our work lives to cultivate relationships and undertake pursuits that nourish our spirits and give real meaning to our lives? Each indicator has six or eight subsets or criteria that reflect our health in each category and are used to calculate a total score. Taken together, the Canadian Index of Wellbeing indicators provide Canadians with a powerful tool we can use to design public spaces and deliver public services that nourish our individual and collective happiness. We can define exactly what it takes to make ours truly the smart and caring nation we dream of, and then measure our progress.

Statistically, happily yours,
David

John F. Helliwell is an officer of the Order of Canada, professor emeritus of economics at the University of British Columbia, and Arthur J.E. Child Foundation Fellow of the Canadian Institute for Advanced Research. He has used his academic career to study well-being in its social context and incorporate well-being into economic models. A prolific researcher and writer, he has served as a research consultant to several royal commissions and federal departments, and as editor of the *World Happiness Report*, a landmark survey of the state of global happiness.

Free from Violence

End violence against women in Canada.

To Tracy Porteous

Dear Tracy,

A wise person said one of history's most useful tasks is to bring home to us how keenly, honestly, and painfully past generations pursued aims that now seem to us wrong or disgraceful. Canadians in generations to come will look back at us today with disgust and even horror as we permitted countless women in our country to suffer the physical wounds and mental trauma of violence, intimidation, and fear. I have no doubt of that. I'm reminded of this painful fact each year when the recipients of the annual Governor General's Awards in Commemoration of the Persons Case are honoured. These are happy occasions to celebrate each year the remarkable achievements of a distinguished group of Canadian women. And these are truly happy occasions. Your smile lit up the room when you received the award in 2014. Yet these moments are also tinged with sadness and regret. Without fail, many of the award winners – you among them – are recognized for their deep and ongoing involvement in ending violence against women and helping women and their children who are victims of violence. The award winners work to strengthen the laws we use to combat violence against women. They advise governments on actions we must take to reduce the number of violent acts against women. They support women who are victims of violence by ensuring these women and their children get the basic necessities of life – food, clothes, and shelter. They strive for greater equality for women, recognizing that inequality in condition is the greatest underlying cause of violence against women.

The work and achievements of the honourees are noble. Yet the need for their existence blights our nation. Violence takes the lives of many thousands of women each year worldwide. Harassment, intimidation, and fear rob us of the full contributions of many thousands more who are forced to endure diminished lives. When women and girls must avoid certain situations out of fear, their lives are diminished. When women and girls are harassed in person and on-line, their lives are diminished. When women remain in abusive relationships because of intimidation or out of concern for the welfare of their children, their lives are diminished. When women's lives are diminished, our country is a lesser place in which to live. Some will argue that the lives of women are better in Canada than in most other countries. True. But this fact is of little comfort to the women and girls in our country who are nonetheless victims of violence, intimidation, and fear.

One of our finest characteristics as Canadians is that we never shy away from learning the truth about ourselves collectively – good and bad. We are not a people who tell pleasant lies to ourselves. Our national mission for the next generation, therefore, should be to strive with all the effort and resources at our disposal to eliminate all forms of violence, intimidation, and harassment directed at women in homes, schools, workplaces, streets, neighbourhoods, and on-line. It will be the single biggest step we can take to make our country smarter, more caring, and more just. We should achieve this goal for our country and ourselves. What an incalculable waste of potential we suffer because many girls and women endure lives constrained by violence and the threat of violence. On a more fundamental level, it is simply the right thing to do. Canadians may be free and equal under the law, but laws alone are not enough to stop violence and ensure genuine equality. We will never be fully free and equal until all women in our country are truly free from violence and the threat of violence. We should also pursue this goal to inspire others. Canada can be a beacon to the world of what full freedom truly looks like.

We can start by making all Canadians aware of the problem and its magnitude. When we shine our brightest light on this problem, we make it more visible, bringing us closer to taking the actions we must take to eliminate violence and the threat of violence against women. We can then educate all

Canadians – as you have been doing for many years – on these very actions. Especially men. All men need to play a fundamental role in increasing awareness and taking action. Some men are the criminals who commit violent acts against women. Some men are the bullies who seek to intimidate women. Some men are the predators whose actions and words instill fear in women. Some men are the silent witnesses to acts of violence, intimidation, and harassment against women. All good men must be leaders who, through their words and deeds, spur Canadians of both sexes and every age to reach the high and worthy goal we set.

Canada is a beloved country – one to cherish. We have much to praise, much to celebrate, much to share with the world. Yet our nation has failed far too many women. We should make it our goal never to fail another girl or woman again.

Thank you for being a stalwart in this mission.
David

Tracy Porteous is a registered clinical counsellor in British Columbia who has spent more than thirty years working to stop violence against women and girls in her home province, across Canada, and around the world. In October 2014, she was one of five women honoured with the Governor General's Award in Commemoration of the Persons Case.

Expecting Excellence

Pursue excellence as well as equality of opportunity.

To Paul Davidson and Denise Amyot

Dear Paul and Denise,

Can we have equality of opportunity and excellence, too? That's the question asked famously by John W. Gardner, who was United States secretary of health, education, and welfare at the height of President Lyndon Johnson's efforts to create the Great Society in his country. I've spent a career pondering this question. I've concluded we *must* have both, because we can't truly have one without the other. I'm also persuaded we *can* have both. Excellence flourishes when the fullest number and range of people are able to pursue it and in doing so continually raise all of our aspirations and expectations to a higher standard. On the flip side, equality of opportunity is a devalued currency if we don't use it to pursue excellence. Equality of opportunity *or* excellence, then, is a false choice. They are complementary, mutually reinforcing qualities, not mutually exclusive or excluding. Yet they don't necessarily advance in parallel. Life is never that simple. We are a people who cherish equality and pursue it in status, rights, and opportunities. No nation has worked harder than ours to make opportunities available to the full spectrum of our people, including our newest citizens. What about excellence today? The greatest challenge Canadians face today is complacency. We don't draw nearly enough inspiration from the central tenets of excellence: a relentless drive to unravel and demystify, a sense of mission to improve all about us and, most of all, the dreamer's response to any challenge: "Why not?"

It hasn't always been this way. Consider our early history as Canadians. Wave upon wave of immigrants came to settle in this country, having lost everything but hope. We were French habitants later abandoned by our kings and noblemen, English and Irish without property or background, and Scottish highlanders swept from rude crofts by the Clearances. Equality of opportunity combined with immense challenges of nature inspired these men and women to make enormous achievements – to achieve excellence in their own ways in their unique environment. Then came other Europeans, and Asians and Africans later on – all fuelled only by their wills and their wits. What enormous energy and intellect these human waves imparted to the Canadian frontier and then right to the hearts of our cities! As educators, both of us appreciate and find inspiration in the immigrant experience of James McGill. He came to Canada from Glasgow at age fifteen – penniless, without prospect. He prospered from the fur trade and bequeathed his land on the slope of Mount Royal to found a great university.

This reference to McGill University is not unintentional. Higher education is a prime example of our country's success in pursuing excellence. We have a diverse collection of outstanding colleges and universities that most other countries look to emulate. We have been able to build the research and teaching enterprises of our universities together. In many countries, these disciplines are split. They shouldn't be. We also manage the movement of men and women from school to work much better than most nations do. And we have a system of education that is largely affordable, in part because it's progressive. While we have tuition fees at the post-secondary level, we also have federal, provincial, and institutional schemes that support students according to their need for financial aid. These are important developments we can build on and must share with the world. That's not to say that higher education in Canada is an exemplar of excellence. Some years ago, Al Johnson – whose career saw him serve as an author, professor, civil servant, and president of the CBC – highlighted the gap between ensuring equality of opportunity and pursuing excellence during his examination of federal government support for higher education and research. He said: "We have dramatically increased opportunity for young people of whatever origin to go to college or university. But in the process we somehow or other have lost sight of excellence. We do not have a tradition in this country – an institutional structure – that would lead us in the direction of the American model of excellence. We do not have foundations in this country that traditionally finance a particular faculty or institute. We do not have a tradition of the private sector itself taking an interest in financing this or that particular thing on university campuses."

I've long thought the ideal place to start nurturing an environment of excellence in Canada is with students and our schools. The great thing about Canadian education is how inclusive it is – from kindergarten to post-secondary school. We as Canadians – and our ancestors for generations before us – made a deliberate choice. We chose not to use education to perpetuate elite groups or a ruling class. We believe we make all our citizens stronger by holding open opportunities – especially opportunities to learn – as widely as possible. We should now arm our young people with the ability and expectation to achieve excellence, and then recognize and reward them when they do. Good enough shouldn't and doesn't cut it anymore. Cultivating an expectation of excellence can begin right away and – as these young people leave school to begin careers, start businesses, go into public service, and become leaders – it will soon permeate all aspects of Canadian life. The best way to cultivate this expectation of excellence is by having our colleges and universities recruit and attract the finest students and faculty from around the world. This recommendation may seem counterproductive to some. But to be the best, you must learn with, work with, and measure yourself against the finest in the world. What a curious phenomenon it is that for generations this country sent more of its students to universities abroad than we welcomed as foreign students. A country so welcoming to refugees and new citizens should not put up barriers against foreign students – demanding inappropriately high tuition fees, setting meagre quotas for entry, and placing restrictions on opportunities for summertime or post-graduation work. This bias against outsiders is mimicked in many regional programs as a bias against out-of-province students. I can think of few more damaging barriers to a sense of the richness of Canada in its diversity than the insistence that young people from one region stay in that region for university studies and not mingle with young people in another region. And I can think of no practice more calculated to impoverish our richness and stifle our pursuit of excellence than not making a much greater effort to encourage the finest students from around the world to make their academic homes in Canada.

This openness and spirit of collaboration should also extend to pursuing research excellence. We Canadians are collaborative by nature, and we realize that to achieve a critical mass and scale in research we can't rely on a single institution. By working collaboratively, we can achieve much higher levels of excellence than we would if each of our universities, for example, were on its own. I also think it's easier to combine in partnership a number of institutions, including private-sector organizations, in Canada than in many other jurisdictions. I go back over three decades when Fraser Mustard first began to develop the Centre for Excellence concept in Ontario. Out of that effort came CIFAR, the Canadian Institute for Advanced Research, and then the federal Networks of Centres of Excellence.

The time is ripe for Canada to excel as never before. We live in a period of history characterized by dramatic and sometimes unnerving change. We should take advantage of this fluidity and emerge as a paragon of excellence. One of the periods of the past that is peculiarly fitted to serve as a model of our present age is that most creative period of history that elevated Western civilization from the darkness of the Middle Ages. It was the Renaissance, and Florence was its centre. What was it in the fresh breezes of the Florentine air that fanned such creative sparks? What muse inspired Dante's redesign of the Italian language, Michelangelo's sculptures and paintings, Leonardo da Vinci's paintings and engineering, the Medici family's networks in banking and trade, Machiavelli's ideas on government, and Savonarola's on religion and revival? To adapt Shaw's quote, I suggest it was a readiness to see things and wonder why, and to dream dreams and ask, "Why not?"

This thinking has rested at the centre of the Order of Canada, its motto being "They desire a better country." Honours such as the Order of Canada are an ideal way to recognize men and women who strive for and achieve excellence in a variety of disciplines. During my tenure as governor general, we have made a point of stressing excellence by shining a bright light on Canadian honours – to the point where we revived awards that had lain dormant for years, most notably the Governor General's Caring Canadian Award (now elevated to the Sovereign's Medal for Volunteers) for unsung heroes who volunteer to build better communities across the land. We were further inspired by something Christopher Plummer said to reporters at the Academy Awards ceremony in Los Angeles. When asked what the "snowflake" pin on his lapel represented, the distinguished actor replied that he was delighted to inform everyone that the pin represented the Order of Canada, a prestigious honour of excellence, and that he wore it to remind himself that he must always represent the best of his country when he was abroad. Since then, I have asked Order of Canada recipients to wear their insignia, "the snowflake," with deserving pride, and when others at home or abroad ask what their Order of Canada insignia is, tell them it represents excellence, the desire to build a better country, and tell them what they did to achieve it. Do so not out of arrogance but out of eagerness to inspire fellow Canadians to achieve excellence themselves.

Fifteen hundred years ago, philosopher and theologian Saint Augustine said, "If you wish to judge the quality of a city, look to see what it cherishes." Canadians have long cherished equality of opportunity. We must continue to do so. Yet let us also revere excellence and see to what heights of achievement our reverence takes us.

Your colleague,
David

Paul Davidson is president of Universities Canada, the national voice of ninety-seven public and not-for-profit universities and university degree-level colleges in the country. Denise Amyot is president/CEO of Colleges and Institutes Canada. In their roles, Paul and Denise have centred their efforts on making sure higher education in Canada not only promotes greater opportunities for students but also enables them and all Canadians to strive for and achieve excellence.

The State of North America

Complacency is our enemy.

To Heather Moulton

Dear Heather,

I wonder where I might be today without Longfellow House. I discovered this special place during the autumn of my first year at Harvard. I had a severe case of homesickness in the fall of 1959. Mine wasn't a longing for home; it was more a deep apprehension that maybe I wasn't good enough for the Ivy League, that maybe a working-class kid from a small town in northern Ontario didn't belong at such a prestigious institution of not merely education but also American thinking and culture. Then I found Longfellow House. I happened across this house one block from Harvard Square when I noticed a bronze plaque that read "Henry Wadsworth Longfellow, poet, writer,

Harvard professor lived and worked here. Open to the public." So I went in.

I read there about his famous poem "The Song of Hiawatha." I learned it was a paean to the place where I was raised and featured characters that arose from the same territory as I did. Henry Wadsworth Longfellow's mythic, romantic verse reminded me that I came from a real place, with a distinguished history and richness of experience that are meaningful to even the most sophisticated and erudite. This revelation grounded me, gave me confidence, and filled me with the sense that I was wanted and appreciated even though I was hundreds of miles from my hometown. So I send thanks to you – and to your predecessors – as president of Friends of Longfellow House.

Once gained, I never lost the feeling of belonging I discovered at that historic place, and it is rekindled every time I journey to your welcoming country. I have visited the United States countless times since my years as a student there ended in the early 1960s – as a tourist, educator, and public official. One of my more memorable visits was as a father and grandfather: When my daughter, Alex, was waiting for the birth of her daughter Sadie. Alex and I drove many, many hours through a snowstorm from Toronto to Green Bay, Wisconsin, and back again to bring her daughter home safely. Best road trip ever!

My connection to the United States involves another human link – an all-important one. My mother was born in Sault Ste. Marie, Michigan, where her father worked as a supervisor on the American locks along the St. Mary's River, which joins Lake Superior and Lake Huron. I've always thought these five locks – engineering marvels first built in the late nineteenth century – symbolize the relationship between our two countries: they may be separate, but they run parallel, operate in harmony, and open the Great Lakes basin to the world. In fact, at $5.5 trillion, after the United States and China, the Great Lakes region represents the third-largest trade entity in the world.

I grew up on the Canadian side of the locks in Sault Ste. Marie, Ontario. As a child, I would spend hours watching the huge lake freighters float majestically through the locks and along the river, bringing ore and grain from deep within the continent to the industrial cities of the Great Lakes, the Eastern seaboard, and even Europe. Growing up in the Soo – a physical part of the Great Lakes region and its huge commercial and transportation network – made me feel I had as much in common with people in Duluth, Chicago, Detroit, and Cleveland as I did with my countrymen in, say, Thunder Bay, Windsor, Toronto, and Montreal.

I've been incredibly lucky to be a citizen of this trans-border region. Don Peddie, an executive at the *Minneapolis Star Tribune*, recruited me to attend Harvard in my second year of high school. Don was an alumnus and legendary recruiter of scholar-athletes from throughout the region on both sides of the border. Yet my journey to Cambridge almost never happened – Longfellow House notwithstanding. My high school principal – a good man – refused to write me a reference letter. He thought talented people should stay close to home and serve their community and country. His was a well-intentioned thought but a woefully short-sighted and misguided one, for I had every intention of returning to Canada. Thankfully, two other men thought differently than he. One was the dean of admissions of Harvard College – Bill Bender – who decided the school must be a meritocracy and not an aristocracy, so he dispatched recruiters such as Don Peddie across the continent. The other was my high school football coach, who eagerly gave me the vital reference my principal had refused.

My studies in the United States were a formative part of my life. I learned so much; my debt is so great that I have continued my association with Harvard throughout my life, becoming the first non-American to chair its board of overseers. Many Canadians have stories similar to mine – of having our lives enriched and enlightened by time spent in the United States and with Americans. These experiences highlight the fact that people – individual men and women – matter. We tend to get all tied up into thinking that big departments and agencies and organizations drive growth and prosperity on autopilot. Yet anything positive in life is spurred by two or more people getting together to achieve something much greater than they could do alone.

What we the people of Canada and the United States have accomplished together is remarkable. The proof in the form of trade, jobs, and investment is staggering. Many of our industries operate in harmony. And millions of Canadians and Americans not only work together but also raise families together. My parents are living proof. Right at the time I was at Harvard, a distinguished son of that school, President John Kennedy, addressed a joint session of Canada's House of Commons and

Senate and described impeccably the enduring ties that bind our two peoples. He said, "Geography has made us neighbours. History has made us friends. Economics has made us partners. And necessity has made us allies." Way back then, we defined necessity primarily as our shared need to safeguard ourselves, our friends, and our way of life at the height of the Cold War. I often ponder what chief need animates us today and take guidance and draw inspiration from John Buchan. One of my most illustrious predecessors as governor general, Buchan was also a novelist and historian. He used the final words of his biography of the Scottish patriot Montrose to press home humankind's eternal duty to infuse old truths with new passion. "No great cause is ever fully lost or fully won," Buchan wrote. "The battle must always be renewed and the creed restated."

I think this rallying cry remains alive for us today. Canada and the United States are special. Our countries are the first two nations in the long history of civilization that have been built on an experiment: to test whether all the peoples of the world – regardless of origin, colour, religion, culture, class, and wealth – could live together and grow, build, and prosper. Over our histories, we have met that test with enthusiasm, deepening and accelerating our commitment to pluralism – so much so that many of us take our respective successes for granted. Such complacency is now our enemy. We have inherited a great legacy. We must now restate our creed with renewed passion. We have a responsibility to our citizens, to each other – Canadians to Americans, Americans to Canadians. That duty extends to future generations here at home and to people throughout the world: to work with growing determination to achieve greater security and prosperity, to improve the health of our people and our environment, and to tackle and overcome the most daunting challenges of our times – not just for ourselves but for all the peoples of the world.

My visits with Americans convince me that Canada and Canadians continue to be valued partners. The cross-border ties between friends, families, business people, and cultural associations are thick and strong. These people-to-people ties are vital assets for both our countries. Although our relationship is strong, we cannot take this relationship for granted and must attend to it continually. By fighting complacency and nurturing an ever-healthier rapport, not only are we better placed to address irritants, but we also equip ourselves to pursue unprecedented opportunities. Our scientists, researchers, investors, entrepreneurs, and business people must build the partnerships we need to regenerate rusted cities, rejuvenate physical infrastructure, move beyond the internal combustion engine, retool our schools for the economy of the future, and help those in need enjoy lives of dignity and meaning. To do so, we must deepen the existing bonds between our two nations. Not just by doing more of what we have always done, but also by searching to expand our relationships in wholly new ways. Not just between businesses, but also between businesses and schools and research organizations and philanthropic groups. We must broaden our partnerships beyond the conventional and into the truly extraordinary.

Insecurity was my enemy many years ago when I first walked through the doors of Longfellow House. That wonderful home that you now preside over dispelled my destructive sense of inferiority. Today, complacency is our shared enemy. Let's defeat that adversary in the same way: by reminding ourselves that we come from this magnificent shared land which has given us so much; by reminding ourselves of our history – both sorrowful and triumphant – together on this continent; by reminding ourselves of the richness of our shared experience and the thick and strong bonds we have forged over many, many generations. Those bonds certainly include the verse of Longfellow, not only "The Song of Hiawatha" but also "Evangeline," his epic poem about the Great Expulsion of the Acadians from New Brunswick, Nova Scotia, and Prince Edward Island. Let's remember it all and use it to build the smart and caring world we dream of.

Thank you.
David

Heather Moulton was president of the Friends of Longfellow House – Washington's Headquarters. Located one block from Harvard Square at the edge of Harvard University Yard in Cambridge, Massachusetts, Longfellow House was the long-time home of Henry Wadsworth Longfellow, the celebrated nineteenth-century American poet and Harvard professor. Longfellow acquired the stories from which "The Song of Hiawatha" is composed in Sault Ste. Marie, where Lake Superior flows into Lake

Huron, from the local North West Trading Company manager. The manager was married to an Ojibwa princess, who recounted to him the oral history of Hiawatha in Ojibwa, which he transcribed into English and gave to Longfellow on a chance meeting while Longfellow was voyaging on the Great Lakes. Operated by the United States National Park Service, Longfellow House also served as headquarters for General George Washington during the siege of Boston in 1775–1776.

Faith in Canada

Do not take religions as absolute truths.

To Andrew Bennett

Dear Ambassador Bennett,

Victor Hugo wrote that "a faith is a necessity to man. Woe to him who believes in nothing." I'm a man of faith and, given our shared concern on matters of faith, I feel compelled to share my thoughts with you. My faith is based in love: some power greater than us put us all here on this earth to serve others and help improve their lives. To love others, we must first understand and respect ourselves. Only by recognizing our own individual worth can we help others realize and fulfill their own.

My faith is the guiding influence of my life and the lives of many Canadians. It's also a powerful force in enabling communities large and small – especially families – to function in a healthy way. My faith, then, isn't influenced by anything magical or miraculous. Even though I've had modest training to be a lay reader in the Anglican Church and I'm a regular churchgoer, I tend not to get caught up in the doctrinal aspects of religion. To me, church is a way to connect with friends and neighbours to get a sense of the views of others and to be reminded of the primary power of love. (I've been known to text my daughters the highlights of our priest's sermons. No live-tweeting so far.) Yet belonging to one church has never stopped me from reaching out to people of other denominations or faiths. When I served as president of the University of Waterloo, we lived near a faith-based Mennonite settlement and became close to many people in that community. I took part in several barn-raisings and regularly drove the tractor for the farmers at harvest time each year.

While I leave religious doctrine to the experts, I still find myself having lively discussions about it with my daughters. They usually win: Man made God; God didn't make Man. My response to most of their highly rational arguments usually ends up being a variation of "This isn't a question of reason, my dear; it's faith." Although my daughters often get the upper hand in our arguments over doctrine, I've found my simple faith to be a reliably true moral compass. That compass points to humility. Humility in the sense that I don't have all the answers, religions don't have all the answers, and no one religious faith is absolute. Humility also means I am no better than anyone else: we are all deserving of love, mercy, and grace – from whatever power put us here and, more importantly, from each other.

This way of looking at life applies to people of all faiths or of no faith.

I've also found that when I approach decisions from the perspective of serving others in a spirit of humility, nearly all my life's decisions have been easy to make. At the start of my sophomore year at Harvard, in 1960 before the U.S. civil rights movement began to flourish, I was considered for membership in one of the school's final clubs. These are a handful of social clubs for undergraduates. A fellow student from Nigeria was also under consideration for membership. I was accepted; he wasn't. Members on the selection committee said their decision wasn't based on any racist beliefs they held personally. They denied entry to the Nigerian student because they believed club alumni, who supported the club financially, wouldn't be happy if a black man were made a member. I resigned from the club when I learned about the committee's decision. Mine was no act of high-minded protest designed to spur a revolt against racism in final clubs or in the school. I just wasn't comfortable being part of that kind of organization: membership in it would be inconsistent with my faith and moral compass.

While my decision wasn't difficult, it did have consequences. I began to realize more fully something about myself that I had sensed but didn't completely understand. Without being moralistic or, I hope, too *precious*, I noted simply that my centre of gravity often pointed me to a road less travelled. At about this time I took the basic training to become a lay reader in the Anglican Church. In that role during several summers, I relieved the regular minister at two churches on reserves near my own hometown on Sundays when he was on vacation. Two roommates (varsity basketball and baseball players respectively) and I chose not to go into the residence (at Harvard, Winthrop House) preferred by the athletes but another residence frequented by keen students generally doing undergraduate theses for their honours' degree and all aspiring to graduate studies. On our hockey road trips, I always had a book to finish or an essay to prepare and I didn't hang out much. I trained rigorously so chose to pass on the regular parties.

I wasn't elected to be captain of the Harvard varsity hockey team at the end of my junior year. I had been freshman captain, was selected to the All-American team, named most valuable player, and appointed acting captain by our coach during my junior year when our captain was injured. Most of my teammates viewed me as a bit of a different cat. While I was passionate about hockey, I was also a student who believed in working as hard in the classroom as I did on the ice. I didn't consider myself to be a wronged guy. I simply made the only decision I was comfortable making. When your faith is founded on serving others and your moral compass points toward humility, I've found most every decision is an easy one.

My commitment to my faith was reinforced when I represented Canada at the Mass to celebrate the election of Pope Francis. His Holiness used his homily to call on all people to care for each other. His was a message that transcends all religious faiths, ethnic nationalities, and geographic borders. And it was received as such: people from many cultures, countries, and languages raised their voices in unison to support the words of the new pontiff. I was heartened to witness this unity. We live in an age in which religious fanaticism is resurgent and religious zealots use faith to inflame the worst of human passions – intolerance, hatred, and pride. Canada isn't immune to these passions. We have witnessed murderous acts committed by those consumed by religious fervour. We see instances of cruelty and violence committed against people of minority faiths and their houses of worship. And our history is full of examples of organized intolerance and prejudice designed to pit people of one faith against another. One that stands out to me is the Protestant Protective Association. In the 1890s, this political party convinced enough Ontarians that Catholics were taking over the province to elect several members to the provincial legislature. Their first order of business was to try to block French-language education in the province and use any political success in Ontario to thwart French-language education in Manitoba and throughout the west. Imagine that: a group of partisans from a dominant religion trying to impose their faith and language on Canadians of minority faiths and languages. Doesn't sound very Canadian to me.

We have learned – and must continue to learn – from our mistakes. We must never allow our religious beliefs to inspire intolerance, hatred, and pride. Our faiths should be sources of love, service, and tolerance. They should be our guides and not absolute truths. They should be living faiths that spring from who we aspire to be – smart and, above all, caring people.

Only then can we speak to others with authority. Only then can our country be a true beacon for those of all faiths throughout the world.

Faithfully,
David

Andrew Bennett is Canada's inaugural ambassador of religious freedom. The Office of Religious Freedom was established in 2013 to protect religious minorities under threat, oppose religious intolerance, and promote religious pluralism.

Challenge to Lawyers

Strive for the public good.

To the twenty-seven clerks of the Supreme Court of Canada

Dear Clerks,

When I was a young law dean making my welcoming address to new law students, I often posed this question: "Is law just?" To answer it, we need both to know the law and to possess a sense of justice. I would encourage students always to ask whether the particular law they were working on was just. And, if it was not, I would ask, "What will you do about it?" I would then remind these new students that soon, each of them would swear an oath to "improve the administration of justice." To sharpen their understanding of the distinction between law and justice, I would ask these first-year law students to watch the film version of *To Kill a Mockingbird*.

Set in Jim Crow Alabama, the film hinges on the trial of Tom Robinson, an African-American field hand accused of raping a white woman. All the mechanics of a criminal trial under English common law and the state of Alabama's legal system are followed scrupulously. Yet the trial is a shameful exercise in justice denied – a fact that is visible to all who participate in and attend the trial. The trial and the entire justice system are tools to maintain a racial hierarchy in the state and not a means to strive toward justice.

With this example in mind, I would point out to students that to understand whether a specific law is just, they must know that law well; they must know its history, its reason for being, whether the circumstances of its application have changed, whether its interpretation has altered, and, if need be, what they would do to fix it. To ensure that they measure the law against an appropriate standard, I would urge them to work wisely over the next three years of their studies, and through their entire professional life, to know the law well but also to refine their sense of justice, the yard stick they use to "measure" a specific law. That, after all, is why each of us embarked on the study of law in the first place. The pursuit of justice is noble, idealistic, demanding, and compellingly important for a good society.

I love the law. In my forty-five or so years as a teacher at five Canadian universities and a public servant working in the context of the law, the legal profession has given me many things: a fulfilling career; a way to connect and interact with succeeding generations of Canadians; a medium through which to explore human nature, the state of my country, and the condition of the world; and a method by which to measure and realize justice. I have a strong feeling you love the law, too. You don't become a clerk to a justice of the Supreme Court of Canada without unflagging energy, high intelligence, and, most of all, an intense passion for the law as a discipline, profession, and wellspring of order, fairness, and justice in our country.

When I was asked to serve as governor general of Canada, I had much to learn. Despite my background as a student, professor, and dean of law, I had to relearn the legal principles and conventions of our constitution. My re-education enabled me to develop a deeper admiration for how precious the rule of law is in our country, and how thin and vulnerable its veneer can be. And by rule of law I mean the prevailing legal system in Canada centred upon the constant, relentless pursuit of justice. Law without the striving toward justice is a hollow pursuit. The rule of law married to the constant search for justice is what makes us as citizens free. Indeed, as the old saying goes, law is the rules that make people free. When we think of the law as a way to strive toward justice and serve the good of citizens, we need to ask ourselves an obvious question: How do we improve the law to make justice more abundant and pronounced, and freedom more secure and widespread?

When I consider the need to constantly strive for justice through improvement, Hugh MacLennan's analogy comparing gardens to civilizations comes to mind. His words – from his novel *Voices in Time* – are worth quoting in full: "In the relatively rare periods in the past that we call civilized, people understood that a civilization is like a garden cultivated in a jungle. As flowers and vegetables grow from cultivated seeds, so do civilizations grow from carefully studied, diligently examined ideas and perceptions. In nature, if there are no gardeners, the weeds that need no cultivation take over the garden and destroy it."

As gardeners in the field of law, we must always be looking for ways to improve the quality of our profession and ourselves as lawyers. A good place to start our work is by looking at the current definition of professionalism in the law. I am a member of the Ontario Bar, so let's begin here. In Ontario, new members swear an oath: "I accept the honour and privilege, duty and responsibility of practising law as a barrister and solicitor in the Province of Ontario. I shall protect and defend the rights and interests of such persons as may employ me." It continues: "I shall neglect no one's interest. . . . I shall not pervert the law to favour or prejudice any one. . . ." and, of overwhelming importance, "I shall seek to improve the administration of justice." We see important duties reflected here to the client, justice, and the public interest. This series of duties is consistent with the principle of peace, order, and good government that underpins our concept of the good society in Canada.

One of the best modern reformulations of professionalism in the law is the American Bar Association's Model Rules of Professional Conduct: "A lawyer, as a member of the legal profession, is a representative of clients, an officer of the legal system and a public citizen having special responsibility for the quality of justice." The ABA's Professional Committee is even sharper: "A professional lawyer is an expert in law pursuing a learned art in service to clients and in the spirit of public service, and engaging in these pursuits as part of a common calling to promote justice and public good." These obligations – to clients, the public, and justice – constitute the social contract that legal professionals have with their fellow citizens and country. All professions have their own social contracts, and each is made up of three principal elements. First, the profession is characterized by specialized knowledge that is taught formally and obtained by experience and under supervision. Second, the state gives the profession a right to have a monopoly and to control entry and exit standards and competence and, to some degree, fees. Third, the profession has a responsibility to society to serve beyond the needs of specific clients. Ours is no different. As legal professionals, we enjoy a monopoly to practise law. In return, we are duty bound to serve our clients competently, to improve justice, and to work to fulfill the public good. That's the deal. What happens if we fail to meet our obligations under the social contract? Citizens, through their elected representatives, will change that social contract and redefine professionalism for us. Regulation and change will be forced upon us – quite possibly in forms that diminish or remove our self-regulatory privilege.

This is not an abstract discussion. As lawyers, we face a profound challenge to our profession. We live in rapidly changing and increasingly complex times. Information is instantly available and in vast quantities via multiple media, making our decisions increasingly difficult. I like to illustrate the pace of change today with the following comparison: it took three centuries for the printing press in Western Europe to reach a majority of the population and reinvent that society; it took the Internet only ten years from the turn of the century to reach a majority of the world's population. The legal profession is not immune to changing conditions and, most of all, changing demands and expectations from the Canadian public. In this light, we must be willing to embrace and adapt to change. To put our test more clearly, we must scrutinize our social contract to ensure that we continuously strive for justice and the public good. You are a key member of the generation that must confront and overcome this challenge. I'm confident you're up to the task, applying the same energy, smarts, and passion that have taken you so far already. As you take up this challenge, let me suggest and explore six key relationships that lawyers have. Each of them causes some friction; I will dwell mainly on those instances of friction – sometimes as stories – in the hope that they will be a catalyst for the good. Remember, the oyster requires the irritation of a grain of sand to produce a pearl.

First, what should be the relationship between the lawyer and justice? One of Canada's early and significant chapters in the story of law clashing with justice took place in Halifax. In 1835, Joseph Howe won a landmark case in the struggle for a free press in Canada when he successfully defended himself against a seditious libel charge brought by members of the powerful Halifax Family Compact. In his newspaper, *The Novascotian*, Howe had publicly accused the ruling class of profiting at the expense of the people. Although he had broken the libel law of the day, Howe was acquitted after he presented proof of his assertions in his famous five-hour defence in the Nova Scotia Legislature. John Ralston Saul recounts this episode in his book on Lafontaine and Baldwin, noting that Howe's argument tackled the question of loyalty versus treason. Howe was called a traitor for telling the truth, and were it not for the strength of his argument, he would have been found guilty under the law. Fortunately for us, Howe persuasively made the case for justice and reform, telling the court, "The only questions I ask myself are: What is right? What is just? What is for the public good?" Howe asked himself the same question I used to ask new law students – "Is the law just?" – and he concluded that it was not. His history-making stand reminds us that we must continue to ask ourselves this question throughout our careers.

The pursuit of justice isn't the stuff of history only. A contemporary instance in which the administration of justice cries out for improvement is the administration of our courts themselves. The Ontario court system has been slowed by an inordinate number of unproductive appearances and some of the longest court delays in the country. In his study of court processing times across Canada, criminologist Anthony Doob found that in cases where no bench warrants were issued, Ontario had three times as many cases lasting more than eight months than did Alberta. And Alberta doesn't exactly stand at the top of the list of expeditious standards of court administration. Ontario has made progress in reversing this trend, with the Justice on Target program and initiatives such as Streamlined Disclosure, Meaningful First Appearances, and Dedicated Prosecution, but the pace is still woefully slow.

Although I have focused on court delays in Ontario, wide discrepancies exist all across Canada, both in our criminal and civil justice systems. A recent World Justice Institute study ranks Canada ninth out of the twelve European or American nations surveyed on access to civil justice. Anthony Doob suggests that reducing these delays would require a hard look at what he calls "court cultures"; that is, "shared expectations about how things should work" among judges, the accused, defence counsels, Crown attorneys, and legal aid. In addition to understanding these cultures, we need a shared willingness to work toward ensuring a fair, equitable, and speedy end to each case, for the benefit of the individuals involved, the legal system itself, and society as a whole. We need to bring a sense of urgency to that shared culture and redefine professionalism. We in the legal community have a responsibility to take the lead in reforming the court system for the public good; remember our oath to "improve the administration of justice," and that justice delayed is justice denied. Or, as Joseph Howe pointed out, "He who delays or withholds justice excites discontent and sedition; [the King] would tell them that they were the rebels."

The lawyer also has a relationship with trust. Trust occupies several dimensions – for simplicity's sake, I want to focus on the micro and macro levels. At the micro level, trust is determined by how fairly, effectively, and efficiently an individual lawyer serves his or her client. That level of service includes the terms of payment. Trust implies that we are paid for value-added only and not for monopoly rents, and that we constantly seek the most cost-effective solution while striving to make our practices as efficient and fair as possible. At the macro level, trust requires each of us to have an abiding concern for how we are regarded by the public – our partners in our social contract – and how we cultivate our unique professional responsibilities toward the public good. A powerful illustration – albeit a negative one – of the importance of trust is the 2008 economic collapse and the extraordinary collateral damage it caused to Main Street in America and around the world. This debacle reflected poorly not only on financiers but also on lawyers. How many lawyers "papered" the deals that involved fraudulent statements of assets, liabilities, income, and valuations? How many lawyers "sounded the alarm" about conflict of interest in the web of financial transactions and creative financial instruments? How many lawyers were silent in the face of a pattern of deregulation that left the U.S. economy naked to excessive leverage – and which any thoughtful observer knew was bound to have its inevitable pendulum swing? And what is especially surprising is that we had a precursor seven years earlier: the dot-com crash of 2001 involving Enron and WorldCom and others, which brought in the Sarbanes-Oxley regulating framework of mind-numbing rules as opposed to principles for judgement. This framework was very costly and of questionable effectiveness at the micro level. At the macro level, it encouraged an even greater system of excess to fall into place. A principal reason why fiscal discipline is so hard in places such as Greece and Italy today is because trust between lawmakers and the public has eroded. Many ordinary citizens believe it is the greed of lawyers, bankers, and accountants that has brought their economies to their knees. Trust must also exist between the lawyer, the public, and institutions such as the Canadian Bar Association and provincial and territorial law societies. Citizens must know effective and transparent measures are in place to resolve their complaints; they must trust in these institutions to govern the legal profession and be responsive to public need. That's the deal.

The third key relationship is between the lawyer and education, both at the entry level to the profession and throughout a professional lifetime. Here I rely heavily on William Sullivan and his co-authors, who wrote *Educating Lawyers*, as well as *Work and Integrity*, his parallel book on the five professions of law, medicine, engineering, nursing, and clergy. In these works, Sullivan describes the three apprenticeships of the professions: cognitive, practical, and ethical-social. The cognitive is the intellectual aspect of the law – meaning knowledge of the law, its thinking and doctrine. The practical refers to the competent practitioner, while the ethical-social refers to identity and purpose: who are we and why do we do what we do? For lawyers, education formally begins at university. Let me focus only on law school. In my judgement, we have allowed too great a divide to develop between academia and the profession. We don't cure this problem by forcing the profession back in, but rather by making the compelling case that the three years at law school mark the beginning of the journey of preparing professionals with all three apprenticeships. We should not leave the practical and the ethical apprenticeships to the end – articling and the bar admission course. We should start with how we choose an entering class. Beginning in law schools, we need to integrate these three apprenticeships – cognitive, practical, and ethical-social – as one mutually reinforcing continuum. Let me illustrate with two stories from my younger years, during which I struggled to integrate these three apprenticeships and lacked the clarity and wisdom to see then the generalized principles that I see today.

When I was a young law dean almost 40 years ago, we chose an entering class of 150 from more than 2,000 applicants based largely on demonstrated academic merit through undergraduate grades. Since then, the Law School Aptitude Test has been added. These intellectual criteria are essential but should not be exclusive. A better system would continue to use demonstrated intelligence as one filter to select perhaps 600 or 700 potential students from the 2,000 applicants. To select 150 students from this pool of 600, extensive interviews should then be conducted and additional criteria employed to identify qualities for professional responsibility: wisdom, judgement, and leadership; demonstrated excellence in any field; relationships with people; ethical sensibility and depth; and capacity to engender trust. Canadian medicine has evolved in this way. In two of the medical schools I know best (McGill and McMaster), applicants once screened to a final list visit 21 different interview stations over two days. Each station is staffed by two interviewers, who present scenarios for each interviewee's response, which can last anywhere from five to ten minutes. Using this method, the admissions committee has 42 different points of view on choosing each student for an entering class. This approach recognizes that the teaching of professional responsibility begins on day one of the university-based M.D. degree. The medical school is also close to the teaching hospitals, and students see patients early on in their education. On top of that, as student members of the profession, they participate in the "white coat" ceremony in their first term, underlining the fact that they are responsible for and to their patients right from the beginning.

As to curriculum in law, I would integrate the bar admission course with the university degree course similar to what medicine does. I would place a broad and extensive focus on ethics in law school to help aspiring lawyers develop a greater understanding of the ethical implications of a proposed course of action and to see their role as public trustees. I would also intersperse internships or articling throughout the academic years and would pair academic and practising lawyers co-teaching each course as much as possible in the curriculum to integrate the three apprenticeships. Let me illustrate what I'm driving at with another anecdote. Perhaps the best experience I had as a law teacher was to help develop a cluster in corporate law and finance at the University of Toronto Law School in the early 1970s. Frank Iacobucci and I were young law teachers. We were lucky enough to pair with Jack Blaine at McCarthy's and with Purdy Crawford and Jack Ground at Osler's. Frank, as I'm sure you know, went on to distinguish himself in many law-related spheres. Jack Blaine was then counsel to the committee to reform the Ontario Business Corporations Act and completed his career as a leader of the corporate bar. Jack Ground also was a leader in the bar admission course, later a Bencher and an Ontario Supreme Court justice and, though retired, continues in the field of alternative dispute resolution. Purdy Crawford had been counsel to the Kimber Committee to reform Ontario securities law and then continued on as a leader in corporate law and business. His most remarkable and last entrepreneurial task was to successfully resolve the claims of holders of Canadian asset-backed securities following the collapse of that market. As young law teachers, Frank and I profited enormously from this experience. And so did our students. This cluster helped establish the University of Toronto in corporate law teaching and practice and in law reform. Frank, Purdy, and both Jacks are the finest of role models. They all lived the three apprenticeships, with the third role – that of public trustee – especially pivotal in their extracurricular law reform work.

I raised medicine a little earlier as a source of guidance. Medicine has many lessons to teach us about the redefinition of the professional. By marrying the professional and academic experiences and by combining theory and practice, the framework for lifelong research, continuous evidence-based education, and professional renewal has been established. All these responsibilities are assumed by the medical school itself, which is built around the hospital and clinical practice. And bear in mind, the first of the three elements of professionalism in the law is specialized knowledge constantly enhanced to improve justice. The symbiosis of the university and the profession is close.

The fourth key relationship is between the lawyer and social need. The law is not accessible for many people today, save for large corporations and desperate people at the low end of the income scale charged with serious criminal offences who receive legal aid. We must engage our most innovative thinking to redefine professionalism and regain our focus on serving the public. We can achieve this goal in many ways. Four come quickly to my mind: avoid the tort law morass of U.S. law; simplify legal procedures and render them more cost-effective; examine the scope of practice to unbundle activities that do not require legal professionals and work with paralegal associations to enhance their competencies; and move the industry standard of pro bono work, including cases, teaching, and law reform, from the current rate of less than 3 per cent to 10 per cent, and build these "honourable hours" rigorously into the firm's revenue structure. If we wish to avoid having change forced upon us, we must embrace such new ideas and innovation.

Let me illustrate this point with a medical story that is set out in Richard Cruess and Joseph Hanaway's history of McGill medicine in the nineteenth century. All Canadians should know of Dr. Thomas Roddick, for whom the McGill entrance gates are named. After studying medicine at McGill, Roddick went to Scotland where he graduated in surgery at the University of Edinburgh. There he studied under Joseph Lister, who was a pioneer in the use of carbolic acid to disinfect the operating room. Lister was so convinced of the medical benefits of carbolic acid as disinfectant that he damaged his hands and lost his ability to operate. Roddick returned to McGill to open a third operating room alongside the two senior professor surgeons who had taught him at McGill before his Edinburgh enlightenment. In his first two years of practice, his patients' mortality rate from surgery was less than 2 per cent annually, all because of the disinfecting power of carbolic acid, with which he bathed his operating room. The two senior surgeons – who refused to use carbolic acid in their operating rooms – saw mortality rates of more than 20 per cent among their patients due to cross-infection. At this point, Dr. William Osler, then a young McGill professor (who later wrote *Principles and Practice of Medicine* – which went through more than forty editions – and became the Regius Chair of Medicine at Oxford), intervened and threatened to publish the comparative statistics in the local newspapers if the two senior surgeons persisted in their refusal to use carbolic acid. They relented, and mortality rates dropped accordingly.

As legal professionals, we can learn several lessons from this anecdote that we can apply to our own profession. First, the story illustrates clearly the importance of using best practices from other jurisdictions and of being open to the ideas and energy of younger members of the profession. As I frequently say, minds, like parachutes, work best when open. Second, the most senior and respected members of our profession must be prepared to intervene to ensure the public good. Third, we must create a culture of constant renewal and continuous improvement in practice and evidence-based learning. Fourth, we need to ask ourselves what the public expects and what members of the public would say if they really knew what was going on in our profession. And fifth, we have a compellingly urgent need to keep the public good foremost in our minds.

The next relationship the lawyer has is with the firm. Earlier, I mentioned the internal social contract within the profession. This contract also speaks to how firms treat their members and staff. Let me illustrate a key aspect of this contract, of which there are many. Our first obligation as professionals is to ensure that a firm allows for its people to enjoy a reasonable balance between work and life beyond work. We shouldn't penalize those with families; we should support them so that they are able to succeed in the field while supporting the most important aspect of their lives: their spouses and children. If we wish to draw from the entire nation's talent pool in attracting our most promising young people of both sexes into our profession, we must find a better balance and strive to keep employees motivated and fulfilled. I am the father of five daughters, of whom the eldest three are lawyers and parents with seven children among them. I have witnessed their courage with amazement and, at times, incredulity as they have built both their careers and their families. And they have done so in spite of their firms. In my professional lifetime, I have seen the shift from having one woman in my graduating law class to a majority today, largely because of the ability, tenacity, and application of women. Yet something happens in firms just as many women are contemplating families, with or without supportive husbands (and the firms are hard on supportive husbands, too); the harsh scorecard is how few firms count women among their senior partners. The women lawyers in firms simply disappear along the way. The good news is we're seeing progress in law schools. Last time I checked, seven of the nineteen Canadian law school deans are women.

I believe the lawyer also enjoys a relationship with public service. Lawyers are particularly well prepared for public service and yet we're substantially under-represented in it. Let me illustrate with my own case. I was all set to commence articling for a career in law in 1965 when my dean asked me to join the law faculty as a teacher. I took a one-year leave of absence from my law firm; this leave of absence is now in its fiftieth renewal! Purdy Crawford, to whom I was to be articled, once ended a letter of reference for me by saying: "You'll be lucky if you can get this man to work for you." The reality is, I've never worked! I enjoyed university life so much I never left until I was in my seventieth year, when I was asked to join the public service. I often say that all of the important things in life I have learned from my children, and all five are in the public service. So I followed their example. And I am very grateful I was given that one-year renewable leave of absence.

We as a profession have traditionally done well in our appointments to the Bench. For the most part, we have an extremely high level of competence and trust and – to the credit of our profession – our most accomplished colleagues are prepared to reduce their level of compensation to join the public service. We must guard and build on this precious tradition of competence and integrity on the Bench.

It is a precious and fundamental responsibility requiring constant vigilance and only the most worthy among us are elevated to the courts. However, we must do much more to ensure that all other areas of Canada's public service are able to draw from our profession. And we must ensure that the quality of the work, the opportunities, and the function of all professional levels are rewarded and appropriately respected in these areas. Part of the trick is to ensure that prospective law students and lawyers are fully aware of opportunities in the public service, and that we encourage movement back and forth, as Frank Iacobucci, for example, has done. He has served in the academy (professor and dean of law, university provost and president), the judiciary (Federal Court of Appeal and Supreme Court of Canada), public service (deputy minister of Justice), and practice early on with Dewey Ballantyne in New York and now as counsel with Torys. Frank would say each of his experiences enhanced his ability to function on the others.

I referred earlier to William Sullivan's *Work and Integrity*, which discusses the Carnegie Foundation for the Advancement of Teaching's study of the professions of medicine, nursing, law, engineering, and clergy. Think of the magic of that title: *Work and Integrity.* Sullivan issues a clarion call for renewing the social contract between the professions and the wider public they serve. He envisions a new model of professionalism that aims at humanizing modern work and improving the equity and quality of contemporary life. We need our own Carnegie Commission on creating a new model for professionalism in law. To borrow a saying from a sister profession: lawyer, heal thyself. We can do this. Our country has a long history of innovation in the law, dating all the way back to Samuel de Champlain, the first governor – in all but name – of what we now call Canada. In 1608, four members of Champlain's crew staged a mutiny, plotting to murder him. Upon hearing of this treachery, Champlain laid a trap for the four conspirators and captured them – good detective work and law enforcement. Champlain then established a tribunal to act as the court. A formal trial took place. Evidence was heard. The accused were represented and, following due process, were found guilty of their crimes. They were sentenced to death. Although the ringleader was hanged, Champlain tempered justice with another idea for the rest of the mutineers. He recommended they be sent back to France for the King's court to review the sentences; they were eventually pardoned, which was common in those days. In this way, Champlain showed not only swift justice but also mercy. Evidence was heard and a tribunal was convened to decide on the prisoners' fate. In a place where there were no courts, lawyers, or civilization, as they knew it, they were able to handle these crimes with ingenuity and, most importantly, fairness.

The challenge that Champlain met so adroitly is the challenge I set before you, the young leaders – the emerging gardeners, if you will – of our profession. Applying your profound ingenuity and deep sense of fairness – qualities that have taken you so far already – I urge you to scrutinize the social contract of the legal profession with the public and also internally so that our profession is always striving toward justice and always working to serve the public good.

Yours professionally,
David Johnston

Each of the nine justices of the Supreme Court of Canada has three law clerks chosen from among the very top graduating law students around the country. They carry out research, draft bench memoranda, and help justices draft judgements. Their service with the court meets in whole or in part the articling requirements of Canada's provincial law societies as a condition of admission to the Bar. These clerks are an ideal representation of the emerging generation of legal professionals in the country.

What's a Monarchy For?

Ask the useful question.

To Deborah Vuylsteke

Dear Deborah,

I am always eager to write to a fellow teacher. I consider you a peer because I spent much of my career – more than forty years – as a university professor and executive. And while I have a different job now, I'll always remain a teacher at heart. I still rely heavily on the skills I honed in my teaching career, as I carry out many of the same duties – speaking to large and hopefully attentive audiences, sharing my advice with young people, and recognizing notable achievements (although I now note achievement with the red and white ribbons instead of a red pen).

I am always aware that when people meet me in my role as governor general – representative of the Queen of

Canada – they must wonder why our country has a constitutional monarchy at all. I thank you for exploring this important question with your students and for your efforts to integrate study of the monarchy in Canada into regular curricula. I share your enthusiasm (not a surprise, I'm sure) and thought I might weigh in on the question with a few insights of my own – teacher to teacher.

With the principle of the Divine Right of Kings safely now in the dustbin of philosophical history and a number of oppressive monarchical regimes rightly toppled since the French Revolution, we can now see a monarchy as one choice that people can make when they decide how to govern their own affairs and, in particular, how to settle the matter of a head of state without polarizing their countries. What the monarchy gets us or prevents us from getting is therefore a question worthy of serious, ongoing scrutiny. I've found this question is not neatly resolved by simplification; so for instance, reducing the matter to merely whether we should exchange the monarchy for a republican government doesn't seem to lead to much clarity.

Aristotle preferred to look at difficult questions by identifying the root issue of each and asking, "What is it for?" So I like to ask, "What is national government for?" And then evaluate whether Canada's constitutional monarchy meets those needs. Peace, prosperity, opportunity, health, security and defence, and protection of freedoms must be high on the list of reasons to have a national government, and after seventy or so years of watching it in operation, I would say our system has arguably served us better than most other systems have served their own populations.

Let's intensify that evaluation a bit. I am always keen to look back into history to gain a better understanding of the present. When Confederation was an infant idea, the possibility of becoming a republic rather than a constitutional monarchy was loudly debated. We chose the latter not from some patriotic sentimentality toward Great Britain (although some Canadians may well have had that affection), but because it seemed at the time the best structure by which the new nation of Canada could achieve two things. It could assert itself as strong and unique in the emerging theatre of North America, and it could be flexible enough to meet the varied needs of its citizens – original inhabitants and immigrants alike – as those needs evolved.

Looking around then at the totalitarian states such as Russia, few in the 1860s held the naive assumption that monarchies guarantee rights and freedoms. There was also widespread appreciation that republics too can fail their own populations miserably. The most telling example was close to home. For four full years (1861–1865) during the debate about governance of our own country, Canadians watched Americans slaughter each other during a civil war in which 750,000 Americans died at each other's hands, arguably only because their definitions of republic could not be resolved. In Canada, the Fathers of Confederation (a moniker that reminds us all of the patriarchy of the times) argued that republicanism – far more than our constitutional monarchy – required uniformity to thrive, and that maintaining uniformity would inevitably lead to clashes such as the American Civil War. They concluded unanimously that the political divisions of pure republicanism could easily lead to failure of the state.

The ideals of republicanism were also well known and understood. When people of free will are impeded by nothing other than the limit of their imaginations, their unfettered ability to achieve common goals through entirely democratic means is the logical foundation of a system. But our founders wanted a form of government that could inspire allegiance without requiring that everyone believe the same thing. It was an early nod to the principle of pluralism that makes this country so pleasant to live in. Indeed, at the outset, it was appreciated (not always warmly) that the constitutional monarchy would allow the provinces unprecedented local control over their own affairs – so much so that the debate rages on (as it did then) about who should be in charge of what. The resulting Confederation is a dynamic unique to Canada in its dimension and proof to me that our system of government has in no way restricted the rights of our citizens to have control over their own affairs. Quite the opposite. It's loud, it's messy, and it's fundamentally democratic.

I've also had the opportunity of late to see how the involvement of the Crown through its representatives nationally and in every Canadian province can inspire the best by recognizing the best. Our orders (such as the Order of Canada, the Order of Military Merit, and the many provincial orders) and our decorations (among them military valour, bravery, and meritorious service) are a system of recognition that, because it carries the authority of the Crown, stands above the level of politics, as it celebrates the very character of the people who inhabit, nurture, and shape this country. I like especially how novelist Robertson Davies expressed this idea. He wrote, "In a government like ours, the Crown is the abiding and unshakeable element; politicians may come and go, but the Crown remains and certain aspects of our system pertain to it which are not dependent on any political party. In this sense, the Crown is the consecrated spirit of Canada."

We have seen throughout our history this spirit of the Crown and its representatives in action – how it has a power that focuses public attention on that which unites us, that which should be celebrated, that to which we should pay attention and, in the process, how this spirit helps us develop our communities and build our nation. I have also learned firsthand over the last handful of years how much this gentle but critical spirit within our constitutional monarchy is respected and cherished.

That's what I think a monarchy is for. My thanks to you and your students for considering such a useful question. Now let the debate rage on!

Fondly and with deep thanks,
David

Deborah Vuylsteke is a history teacher at St. Pius x High School in Ottawa. She has worked with officials at Rideau Hall to uncover the best resources and methods to illuminate for her students the role of the monarchy in Canada. The red and white ribbons Mr. Johnston refers to are those of the Order of Canada.

Thirty Thousand Kids

Resolve Canada's adoption crisis.

To Laura Eggertson

Dear Laura,

Right at the top of my favourite personal characteristics is the fact that I'm a grandfather. My wife, Sharon, and I have twelve grandchildren. Our first two grandchildren are Emma and Téa. My eldest daughter, Debbie, and her husband adopted them from an orphanage in Colombia. I can't imagine our family without them.

On one of our state visits to Latin America and South America, these two wonderful girls joined us in Colombia – their home country. The trip was the most memorable and rewarding of my tenure in that office, because it enabled Sharon, Debbie, and me to experience the girls' native land and its people with them right by our side and also to see it through their eyes. (I should point out that Debbie covered her expenses and those of the girls when they accompanied us.) Our journey together also achieved something I didn't think could be possible: it brought our family even closer together. So no one has to convince me about the benefits and blessings of adoption.

My family's experience gives me insight and some authority on adoption in Canada. Before becoming governor general, I chaired Ontario's Expert Panel on Infertility and Adoption. My work on the panel and my direct exposure to adoption since has led me to the following conclusion: we are failing many children in Canada. The statistics on adoption in Canada tell a harrowing story: some thirty thousand kids are legally eligible for adoption in our country; 41 per cent of young people in Canada's various child-welfare systems have had at least one run-in with the country's criminal justice system; 44 per cent of the kids in provincial and territorial child-welfare systems graduate high school; and a mere 5 per cent go on to post-secondary education (both figures I recall are well below the average rate); children who enter our country's child-welfare systems at age five and younger have much higher rates of mental illness and suicide attempts than other children; 68 per cent of homeless youths are young men and women who have grown out of child-welfare systems without permanent families; and 73 per cent of those who have aged out of the systems are unemployed. The most glaring and troubling statistic – the one from which all other figures flow – is only 7 per cent of foster children are adopted into permanent homes. Ninety-three per cent age out as foster kids.

Our goal as a country, then, is obvious: get these thirty thousand kids out of the insecurity and instability of provincial and territorial child-welfare systems and into durable homes and loving families. This is the best place by far to nurture resilient children and youths who can weather the storms of dislocation and alienation that often lead to mental illness, drug and alcohol addiction, homelessness, and criminal behaviour. The final report of the Ontario expert panel summed up the value of families neatly: "Strong families are the heart and soul of our society. They help give children – the next generation – the best start and provide support as they move through life. Strong families help build strong communities, a prosperous economy and a more secure future."

And yet, thirty thousand kids are without permanent homes, and their risks of living in poverty, having a run-in with the law, suffering from mental illness, and attempted suicide continue to multiply. Some of these kids, of course, will escape these pitfalls and create better lives for themselves, but too many will be compelled to walk down darker paths. I don't wish to lay responsibility for their future at the feet of any one person or organization. Yet Canadians must be honest and admit that our country has an adoption crisis. How should we respond?

We must first understand the problem in its entirety. Child-welfare professionals and organizations compile plenty of data on the many children who are in provincial and territorial child-welfare systems. These data alone aren't enough. These people and organizations need to find out more details about the system itself: How does it actually operate, what kind of performance is it producing, and what factors are contributing to its performance? Gathering this information is hard to do. I know from experience that each provincial and territorial system has its own legal idiosyncrasies when it comes to adoption. What are these quirks, and are they fair and just to children and prospective parents? This elemental question must be answered. When I worked as a law professor, I constantly asked my students to examine systems of laws and individual laws and ask, "Is the law just?" and "Is this particular law just?" I instructed them that they had a professional obligation to rigorously question whether the legal system was keeping pace with our rapidly changing world, and if it weren't, to do something about it. Child-welfare professionals cannot make the laws. Only legislators can. But these pros can speak out and speak up about injustice. They must also look at the support being offered to children in the overall child-welfare system, to those who age out of the system, to foster families, and to adoptive parents. It is vital that the system maintain its support throughout the lives of these children. Those without permanent homes are already at a disadvantage. It is up to the professionals who run our child-welfare systems to ensure the thirty thousand kids don't slide any further behind their peers.

A great way to judge the effectiveness of a system is to compare it with others. What provincial or territorial child-welfare systems within Canada are achieving particular successes in specific ways? Let's identify those systems and those ways and put them into practice everywhere. Likewise, what successful practices being used by other countries can we adapt and implement here? Child-welfare professionals – like any professionals – should never shy away from admitting that there are other, perhaps better, ways of doing things. They must learn best practices from other countries, and from organizations across Canada, for the sake of our children.

We must then work together to uncover answers to the problem. For argument's sake, let us say we know everything there is to know about adoption in Canada. The next step on the road to helping those thirty thousand kids is for us to see things whole and to work together. All the experts and relevant officials in the country must realize that they face this crisis together. They cannot solve their shared problem in isolation. Solutions require open and honest talk, and contributions from all. Collaboration can also have a more immediate effect by creating a concentrated and stable support system. While raising our five daughters, Sharon and I always relied on the kindness of relatives, neighbours, and friends to help us through difficult times. And we, in turn, opened our doors to those in need, including friends of our kids who were dealing with problems at home. Watching my daughter raise her two adopted daughters reinforces for me how essential a strong network really is. It may have become a cliché, but it really does take a village. The kids who are in the child-welfare system lack such a village, such a support system. Those who work in the child-welfare system cannot do it alone. It takes foster families, government officials, educators, social workers, doctors, relatives, good neighbours, and many others to provide a child in care the support he or she needs. But it takes even more than that. These key players not only must be involved but also must communicate with one another and be more aware of what is happening in all areas of each child's life. This reinforcement can act as a net to catch any overlooked problems and help children avoid the hazards of being in care. Members of these support networks also need to listen to the stories of the young people who grew up in the system and to encourage them to share their stories.

We must make sure Canadian parents are part of any solutions. All of us who care about resolving this crisis can start dispelling the myths of adopting older children and informing Canadians of the rewards. The main myth is that older children are unadoptable because they suffer from mental illness or get into trouble or are violent or are too far gone. None of these categories and perceptions is true. Even worse, not only do they prevent children from being adopted, but they also push these young people onto the very path that people expect them to be on. Canadians must be made aware that older kids – just like young children – need the structure of permanent homes and the love of strong families. Canadian parents must be found, drawn out, and shown they have wonderful gifts to offer these thirty thousand kids. At the same time, we must manage the expectations of these parents. Many start the adoption journey without knowing the full story. They look to add a baby to their family and do not consider any other alternative. Yet few newborns are available. The vast majority of the thirty thousand kids in Canada's child-welfare systems are six years old or older. In fact, the average age of an adopted foster child is thirteen.

My family is living proof of the blessings of adoption for adopted children, for parents, for grandparents, for our country. We need to share this blessing ever more widely. Thirty thousand kids in our country are growing up without a place to call home, without a family to call their own. Canada's child-welfare professionals need to understand the adoption crisis in its entirety, work together to uncover answers to resolve it, and galvanize Canadians to get involved in these solutions. We need to resolve Canada's adoption crisis starting now.

Yours sincerely,
David

Laura Eggertson is president of the Adoption Council of Canada, co-founder of the Canadian Coalition of Adoptive Parents, and provincial representative for Ontario on the North American Council on Adoptable Children. She is also an adoptee and the parent of two adopted children. On June 12, 2012, Mr. Johnston awarded her the 2012 Michener-Deacon Fellowship for Investigative Journalism. She is using the fellowship to investigate the health crisis of suicide among Aboriginal youths.

Note: As this book was going to press, the Ontario Government announced a broad package of reforms embracing many of the recommendations of the Task Force Report with the goal of ensuring ambitious increase in the number of foster children placed in permanent loving homes.

From Sea to Sea to Sea

A truly northern nation.

To Major Brian Tang

Dear Brian,

Samuel de Champlain said you really couldn't know Canada until you had wintered over. Four hundred years later, I say Canadians really can't know their country until they've ventured north in winter. And by north I mean to Yukon or Nunavut or Northwest Territories.

Although I have visited the three northern territories a dozen or so times, I had never been truly north in winter until I visited you and your comrades-in-arms at Canadian Forces Station Alert. You all certainly know the true nature of our country. Awed, inspired, and even intimidated by the perpetual darkness and penetrating cold of the polar region in winter,

I was reminded of what Pierre Trudeau wrote after paddling down the Nahanni River in Northwest Territories: "I know a man whose school could never teach him patriotism, but who acquired that virtue when he felt in his bones the vastness of this country and the greatness of those who founded it." Mr. Trudeau is right. We Canadians like to think of ourselves as a northern country. And we are. Yet it is only when we journey to the far north that we truly understand what it means to live in a northern country, what it means to be Canadian.

I received that special lesson in patriotism when I spent two days with the seventy-seven men and women of CFS Alert to learn about the operations and activities of the station, to remember those who perished in two plane crashes nearby, and to attend the change-of-command ceremony that elevated you officially to commander of the station. It was two days of darkness that were full of light – the light of camaraderie, of professionalism, and of service.

I reflect often on those two days and what I learned about the north and therefore about our country. You wouldn't think a mere forty-eight hours could impart such new understanding, but the intensity of my experience at CFS Alert was such that I came away with a deeper appreciation of many things about Canada. I learned about how valuable our presence in Alert and throughout the north is to our sovereignty. That's largely a defensive measure – to safeguard what we spent generations building. The positive feature of our presence is that we have been blessed with this land and this coast, so let's understand it and learn from it and collaborate with others to learn more about the entire circumpolar region. What I learned most about the north is its potential for scientific discovery. What a fascinating laboratory for research and knowledge and understanding this region is! As you know, we've been collecting data in Alert since 1950. We must use it. The circumpolar region is going to be among the first parts of the globe to experience dramatic effects of climate change. Many areas of our north are experiencing these changes already. We must use the data we've amassed and continue to gather to understand and confront the challenge of climate change, and we need to share it with others to increase the scope and speed of our understanding in this vital concern.

I came to realize that our learning must also extend to how we live in the north for, in the end, our greatest resource in the region isn't what lies deep within the ground or beneath the waters, but rather the people with their capacity to collaborate and innovate. I agree with what Mary Simon said about Canada's presence in the region. A woman with a long and distinguished history of service to Canada, especially the north, she stated our north must be built from the inside out. Building from the inside out means nurturing healthy, vibrant, prosperous communities of people. Canada's north is not a mere place on the map – vast, unknowable, empty. It is the living, breathing home to many thousands of Canadians. Inuit, a founding people of Canada, have inhabited the Arctic for thousands of years, and continue to do so today alongside other northerners of diverse backgrounds. This history of human settlement reminds us that, while the world is increasingly aware of the environmental, economic, and strategic importance of the North and of the polar regions, this part of the country is above all home for thousands of people.

If I were a young man with the chance to start my career over again, I would head north. The opportunities to make a substantial contribution to our country are more abundant and pronounced in the north than anywhere else in our country. I can think of no better place in Canada, in the world for that matter, where you can make your mark as quickly and boldly as in the Canadian north. If Horace Greeley long ago told a generation of young Americans to "Go west, young man," I say to today's generation of young Canadians, "Go north, young man and young woman."

We Canadians are fortunate to have many talented, dedicated, and knowledgeable souls living and working in northern communities and building our understanding of this vast and vital part of Canada. The Polar Medal, sanctioned by our Sovereign, Queen Elizabeth II, enables us to do many things in response. It makes it possible for us to celebrate Canada's northern heritage. It recognizes the outstanding contributions made by men and women who live and work in the polar region and Canada's north, which is not without challenges and risks. Recognition through the Polar Medal is a constructive way not only to honour many men and women who achieve excellence, but also to show we place a great value on their achievements and to inspire others to strive toward their own accomplishments in this pivotal region of our country.

I can think of one other way to acknowledge the value we place on the north and on our fellow citizens who make this region their home: we can rethink Canada's official motto. Now it is "*A mari usque ad mare*" or "From sea to sea," which is derived from Psalm 72:8. Shouldn't it reflect the fact that ours is a country that stretches from sea to sea to sea? After all, the plain fact is most of Canada's coastline lies along neither the Pacific nor the Atlantic but along the Arctic Ocean. Shouldn't it proclaim "*A mari ad mare ad mare*" or the plural "*A mari usque ad maria*"? Doesn't that sound better, lovely even? Even more than the beauty of its sound, these words truly reflect our status as a northern nation and give us a standard to uphold and advance, as you and the men and women of CFS Alert do with such professionalism and dedication.

How about it? Canada: *A mari usque ad maria. Canada: From sea to sea to sea* – a truly northern nation.

Thank you, Major, for serving Canada.
David

Major Brian Tang is commander of Canadian Forces Station Alert, the world's most northerly permanently occupied settlement. Located in Nunavut, CFS Alert maintains signals intelligence facilities to support Canadian military operations. The station was established in the early 1950s as part of the Joint Arctic Weather Station. In 1958, Alert began its operational role as a signals intelligence unit of the Canadian Armed Forces. At that time, it became the Alert Wireless Station and was under the command of the Canadian Army. The Royal Canadian Air Force took command of CFS Alert in 2009. It is now a unit of 8 Wing Trenton, Ontario.

Leadership Not Management

Make First Nations education work.

To James Bartleman

Dear James,

An education can be either a wondrous gift or an elusive goal, can't it? I was reminded of these two qualities when I read your memoir of boyhood in Port Carling, Ontario. I delighted in the wonder you experienced as a boy upon entering the library in your hometown for the first time, and how – through the magic of reading books of all kinds – that boy would soon discover the universe was no longer confined to his village. I chuckled when that same boy then wondered what the guys at school would think of him if they learned he had gotten a library card. He decided he didn't care. Your memoir also highlighted the elusiveness of education. A wealthy American summer resident of nearby Lake Muskoka would befriend that same boy – several years older than the one who entered the library – and fund his university study. Now a man, he used his degree as a springboard to a long and distinguished career in service to Canada and Canadians.

Your story struck a chord with me. Just like you, I've seen and experienced the power of education to transform lives and enrich our country. Like you, most of the successes I have enjoyed in my life spring directly from the high-quality schooling I received. And like you, I was a poor, small-town boy who was able to attend a great institution of higher learning as a result of the generosity of others, and then take advantage of that opportunity to strike out on a fulfilling career. I sometimes think about where fate would have taken me if I weren't a scholarship boy. Do you ever wonder what your life would have become without the generosity of that wealthy friend and the education it enabled you to acquire? I imagine you do. Your efforts while lieutenant governor of Ontario and since to encourage young people, especially Aboriginal boys and girls, to read, write, and learn is proof that you haven't forgotten the experiences of that Port Carling lad. Your book program, which has collected more than one million volumes to stock libraries in First Nations communities, particularly those in northern Ontario, is a powerful testament to your understanding of the value of education in all our lives and how it can stem from something as seemingly simple as a visit to the local library. Talk about giving back!

Education has been a personal passion and professional preoccupation of mine for fifty years. I have spent my whole adult life consumed by thoughts that revolve around how men, women, and children gain, enlarge, and wield knowledge. My years as governor general have given me a much different and highly privileged perspective from which to test my ideas and gain a greater appreciation of the history and current state of education in Canada and its value to Canadians into the future. I've concluded we must not be content with the state of learning in Canada. Our education system, while it performs well compared to other countries, is uneven across our country and has considerable gaps. We must make sure people of all ages, regions, incomes, and backgrounds have access to the people, tools, and resources that make education consistently current, practical, and inspiring. I often illustrate the strengths and weaknesses of Canada's public education system by showing an OECD graph that measures the degree to which children in thirty-two countries match or exceed their parents' level of education. In the top four quintiles – the top 80 per cent of the population in level of education – Canada is number one. That is, in Canada, children of the 80 per cent "better educated parents" match or exceed their parents' level of education to a greater extent than any other country. Intuitively, one would expect for the bottom 20 per cent that Canada would stand in the top one, two, or three. We don't. We are in the bottom third of OECD nations. A good part of this gruesome gap is in our Aboriginal population – 4 per cent of our total population with close to 6 per cent of the people in our country under twenty-five years of age. But another sizeable part is made up of deep pockets in inner cities where poor neighbourhoods perpetuate successive generations of poorly educated children. I want to consider the plight of Aboriginal children, though, because the gap is so glaring.

This unevenness and these gaps distress me, because the greatest thing about Canadian education generally over the years is how inclusive it is from kindergarten to post-secondary school. We as Canadians – and our ancestors for generations before us – made a deliberate choice. We chose not to use education to perpetuate elite groups or a ruling class. We believe we make all our citizens stronger by holding open opportunities to learn as widely as possible. This path to success for generations of native-born Canadians and wave upon wave of immigrants hasn't been limited to individuals. Equality of opportunity in learning has enabled whole communities to flourish. Our pioneer ancestors knew its power. They were quick to build churches and schools as soon as the land was cleared and barns and homes constructed. The seed of this wisdom was sown in generations that followed – right up to our very own. At Rideau Hall, we display six paintings by William Kurelek. The panels, *The Ukrainian Pioneer*, depict his pioneer ancestors arriving on the Prairies. Even before they had finished clearing their plot of land and putting a roof on their house, they were building the church and the school. It tells a singular Canadian story.

First-rate public education makes it possible for the majority of Canadians to enjoy personal freedom, intellectual strength, and boundless human potential. Yet this path to success is closed to many Canadians. We lack full equality of opportunity in learning. The calibre of education in some regions of our country falls well below that of other regions. The same holds true for the disparity between many remote as opposed to urban parts of Canada. The resources available to richer districts within metropolitan areas are often much greater than those at hand in poorer ones. Barriers to learning confront visible minorities, new Canadians, and children with special needs. And we fail to recognize quickly and take full advantage of the educational and professional qualifications of recent immigrants. Most troubling is the large segment of children who are failing – through no fault of their own – to use their education as a springboard to personal fulfillment and career success, as we did.

Again, the most persistent and yawning gap that exists in learning in Canada is between Canada's indigenous people and non-indigenous people. This gap is so vast it's a chasm. And it's a problem and challenge that must alarm all Canadians, not just those who directly bear its burden. The rate at which First Nations, Inuit, and Métis students drop out of school is far above that of non-First Nations students – and climbing. This gulf leads me to an inescapable conclusion: education has failed First Nations communities. It has failed Canadians. Most of all, it has failed First Nations boys and girls.

The situation is not much better for those who stay in school. Far too many graduates leave school without the basic knowledge they need to qualify for skills training, let alone go on to college or university. This failure means many young First Nations men and women cannot take advantage of opportunities that enable them to get jobs, start careers, and contribute to the growth and prosperity of their communities. What makes this condition even more troubling is that many young First Nations men and women live in communities located in resource-rich areas of Canada where skills shortages are especially acute. On another level, the glaring inequality in educational outcomes between First Nations and non-First Nations people undermines the inclusiveness of our political and economic institutions – our businesses, governments, and laws. That means it undermines the inclusiveness of Canada, diminishing our country and hobbling it from reaching its full potential.

From past experience – the residential schools bear testimony to this – we know that First Nations communities must play a lead role in developing a system that will succeed. No good reason exists for why First Nations education cannot be as rich as or even richer than non-First Nations education in content and meaning. First Nations children and young men and women have endless amounts of talent, creativity, energy, and drive. So what must we do to ensure fewer First Nations students drop out, more graduate, more get quality educations, and more are prepared to make meaningful contributions to their communities and country? We must first come to grips with the reasons why First Nations education is in such a state: we in Canada are managing an educational system that doesn't work, rather than showing the shared leadership needed to create, nurture, and sustain a system that does work. We must no longer judge our success by how well we manage a system that is so flagrantly not working. When I say we, I mean all of us – First Nations and non-First Nations alike, educators and non-educators, those in our governments and those not in government. I don't point the finger of blame at anyone or any group. I simply want Canadians to arrive at understanding and find solutions. My experience teaches me that solutions are founded on four principles built on bridges to create understanding among us all:

Every decision our schools and school authorities make, every action they take, must be to serve students and to make their education as authentic, accessible, relevant, and broad-minded as possible. The needs of students must be paramount in all decisions; those needs start with being taught by teachers who are passionate about their jobs and qualified to carry out their important duties. Qualifications should include knowing the latest and best methods to teach reading, writing, and math. If teachers do not have this knowledge, they must be taught it. Teach the teachers. Other vital needs of students are safe buildings and stable funding that ensures resources such as quality teaching and safe learning environments are sustainable for years.

All players in the system – elected leaders, public servants, school executives, teachers, you name it – must be encouraged to experiment and take reasonable risks. Encouragement comes through rewarding experiments and risks that produce results, by not penalizing good-intentioned new approaches that fail, and by enabling men and women to share with and learn from their peers what works.

All schools and school authorities must search for partners who share and can help further our mission of building high-quality schools that graduate every single student with the knowledge they need. These partners can range from individual elders to nearby provincial school boards to large private-sector organizations and companies. Partnerships should even include forging relationships with jurisdictions beyond our borders that have found solutions and established practices that could be adopted here. First Nations schools and school boards are building partnerships now with local non-Aboriginal school boards and provincial authorities in New Brunswick and British Columbia. More should.

All officials and organizations involved in First Nations education must hold themselves accountable for the decisions they make and actions they take. For far too long, many of those in charge of First Nations education have not been accountable for results. Again, that is not wholly their fault. It's ours for not demanding accountability from people and expecting results from actions. People and groups who are not held to account for their failings have little incentive to change. Accountability is the engine that drives adaptation, change, and eventually improvement.

You said once that you had a blind faith that you would eventually get a first-rate education. I had that faith, too. Things worked out for us. Yet for many kids, especially First Nations boys and girls, blind faith and good fortune are not nearly enough. And when blind faith fails to reveal and good fortune fails to land, we see the results: half of all First Nations students fail to graduate from high school. This troubling statistic translates inescapably into several others. The unemployment rate for First Nations people living on reserves is some three times higher than that of other Canadians. The average household income for First Nations men and women who live on reserves is less than half that of other Canadians. And suicide rates are up to seven times higher among First Nations youths than for non-Aboriginal youths.

On the flip side, education lies at the heart of everything that is good about life. Armed with a quality education, First Nations men and women are much more likely to enjoy decent jobs, rewarding careers, stable families, prosperous communities, and healthy lives for themselves and their children. Education is no absolute guarantee that First Nations men and women can reach these goals. Yet reaching them without an education is virtually impossible. You knew this truth. You said one time that getting an education was simply a means of pursuing your passions to travel and learn even more. It is scandalous that officials of all governments are not showing the leadership necessary to ensure that First Nations students get the education they must have to pursue passions of their own.

Are we to deny yet another generation of First Nations children the right to the highest-quality education we can possibly give them? Would we sit idly by if any other group of children in our country were given such an inferior education compared to the rest of the country's kids? If Canada is serious about prosperity, innovation, and long-term economic growth, we need to start improving education right away for the fastest-growing section of Canadian society and keep improving it. If we are serious about fairness, equality of opportunity, and simple human justice, top officials of our federal, provincial, territorial, and First Nations governments must really start showing leadership and not management.

That boy from Port Carling, who went on to achieve great personal fulfillment and professional success and who served his country with distinction for decades, was fortunate. Few are. We must stop robbing First Nations boys and girls of the quality education they need to achieve their own versions of fulfillment and success. We must choose leadership over management and start providing them with the kind of education that is their right as Canadians.

Yours in friendship,
David

James Bartleman is a member of the Chippewas of Rama First Nation. He served as an official in Canada's foreign service for nearly forty years and as lieutenant governor of Ontario from

2002 to 2007. An advocate for greater literacy among First Nations, he is the author of four volumes of memoirs and two novels and has earned many awards, including being named an officer of the Order of Canada.

Diplomacy of Knowledge

Create a smarter, more caring world.

To His Highness the Aga Khan

Your Highness,

Award-winning poet and acclaimed constitutional lawyer is an improbable combination of attributes to find in any one person. Frank Scott was both. He had eight volumes of his verse published over his lifetime, and he professed and practised law for many years, arguing several historic cases before the Supreme Court of Canada and serving as McGill University's dean of law. To Scott, law and poetry were not antithetical. They were compatible. A good constitution is like a good poem, he remarked; both are concerned with the spirit of man. Scott's life is an example of how great insight in seemingly disparate disciplines can be combined to generate revealing findings in those disciplines and in entirely different ones. In Scott's case, he combined verse and law to shed light on Canadians and their country and, in that understanding, how they could change their country for the better.

A scholar wrote that the poet and lawyer live harmoniously together in Scott because each speaks with the same humanist voice. I consider your life and work an embodiment of that same kind of harmony. Born in Geneva, you are a citizen of the world. Your many international honours attest to this fact, including your honorary citizenship of Canada and your status as a companion of the Order of Canada. In this way, you abide by Scott's ethos of humanitarianism: "The world is my country; the human race is my race." You're also a spiritual leader, yet you appreciate that the success and indeed survival of our increasingly interdependent world is based on people of many faiths, cultures, and values expressing tolerance, openness, and understanding toward others.

Your belief in the value of working across physical and spiritual borders illuminates our world. The Aga Khan Award for Architecture recognizes the creative design of public facilities and spaces in order to revitalize architecture in Islamic societies. The Aga Khan Development Network partners with a range of public and private organizations around the world to help improve the health, education, governments, and economies of people in developing nations. I think your Global Centre for Pluralism best expresses your understanding of the value of working as widely as possible across physical boundaries and borders of the mind to enhance people's lives. This organization is housed fittingly in Ottawa, the capital of one of history's great pluralist societies. Pluralism is the ultimate expression of working across borders because it recognizes that every person has something meaningful to share to improve the condition of all.

In your address to a convocation audience at the University of Ottawa, you described your way of thinking and acting as "sharing internationally in the hard work of intellectual inquiry." I call your approach the diplomacy of knowledge – different words for the same technique. The diplomacy of knowledge is our willingness and ability to work across disciplinary boundaries and international borders to uncover, share, and refine knowledge. Thomas Jefferson's brilliant metaphor of a burning candle is still, I think, the best way to illustrate the concept of the diplomacy of knowledge and its incredible power. The candle aflame symbolizes not only enlightenment but also the transmission of learning from one person or group of people to another. When I light my candle from the flame of yours, your light is not diminished. Just the opposite: the light from both our candles shines brighter on all around us. In physics, it's called candlepower. The most skilled Western practitioner of working across disciplines is Leonardo da Vinci. A masterful painter, Leonardo's many now iconic artistic works were informed by and express vividly his detailed knowledge of several fields of science: anatomy, botany, geology, engineering, and biomechanics. Conversely, his thousands of pages of notes on science and engineering are brought to life by detailed drawings that perfectly capture his observations, ideas, and designs. Many of these drawings are as striking and famous as his paintings. Leonardo recognized no separation between the arts and sciences. Indeed, he relied on the fusion of scientific theorizing and hypothesizing with artistic expression to interpret and reveal knowledge and thereby advance human understanding.

Few people today have the extraordinary insights and talents of Leonardo. Yet those in businesses, schools, governments, and non-profit groups can surely learn from his example and enhance what their organizations do by cultivating much closer contacts and interactions across disciplines. Two of the greatest incubators of innovation of all time are vivid physical manifestations of the value of interdisciplinary collaboration. At Bell Labs in New Jersey, just across the Hudson River from New York City, leaders were acutely conscious of the need to cultivate teams of specialists from a variety of fields. Some were obvious – physics, chemistry, engineering, mathematics, electronics, and metallurgy. Others weren't so plain – physiology, psychology, and meteorology – but were nonetheless necessary for success. In Silicon Valley, the process of interdisciplinary innovation has been more organic, as a critical mass of engineers, scientists, programmers, entrepreneurs, and investors gradually gravitated to northern California to create less an organization of innovation and more a geographic one – a modern-day, innovation-driven equivalent of Renaissance Florence. Closer to home, Wilder Penfield, one of the first companions of the Order of Canada when it was created on Canada's 100th birthday in 1967 and founder of the Montreal Neurological Institute of McGill University (and colleague of

Frank Scott coincidently), entitled his autobiography *No Man Alone* to illustrate that his early work in mapping the human brain required the weaving together of expertise from many sub-disciplines to see the mind whole. And our subsequent discoveries of how the brain works and how the mind learns have reinforced these interdisciplinary interdependent truths.

The diplomacy of knowledge also requires us to operate across borders. While such actions can be conducted locally, regionally, and nationally, they are most potent when we cross cultural and political borders to cultivate interactions among researchers, scientists, students, investors, and entrepreneurs from many national and cultural backgrounds. When we approach a question from many different cultural angles, we gain a much better sense of its true nature and therefore the best answer. I admire the way you conveyed this very point succinctly in two short sentences at the University of Ottawa convocation: "The affirmation of cultural identity is in no way inconsistent with the idea of encouraging intercultural cooperation. The two movements sustain each other." I compare working across borders to a surveyor and how he or she uses instruments such as a level, transit, and theodolite to determine an unknown point based on known coordinates. The diplomacy of knowledge can be likened to that surveying device. It only makes sense that we take this kind of transnational and multicultural approach. The biggest challenges we face as individual nations are either global in origin or global in scale. Challenges such as ensuring all people can access quality health care services and adequate supplies of healthy food and clean water; guaranteeing people and industries in rapidly developing countries can obtain renewable sources of fuel; and making sure all nations can prosper economically and yet preserve their lands and waters, and mitigate the harmful effects of climate change. Our willingness and capacity to practise the diplomacy of knowledge will determine whether we can effectively tackle these challenges – some of the biggest that human civilization has ever faced.

I think I can say without arrogance that Canadians frequently make excellent partners when it comes to increasing the Jeffersonian concept of candlepower. We have three key qualities in our favour. First, we believe deeply in the intrinsic value of learning from one another and sharing knowledge widely. We came by this belief early and of necessity; the very survival of the first European settlers to Canada was wholly dependent on their willingness to learn from our country's Aboriginal peoples. Second, we've made high-quality education widely accessible to all. By doing so, generations of Canadians have been able to overcome barriers that exist in all countries – racism, poverty, class immobility – and achieve their true potential as individuals. And third, we encourage new Canadians to retain and celebrate those aspects of their heritages that don't conflict with the time-honoured values that have made our country such a success. This balanced approach enriches our country by incorporating the best that others bring. The fact that you decided to house the Global Centre for Pluralism in Ottawa persuades me that you agree with me.

The penchant of Canadians to practise the diplomacy of knowledge is clearly evident in the field of communications. Again, we came to this talent early and of necessity. Our country's vast land mass and sparse population have prompted generations of Canadian engineers, entrepreneurs, and scholars to think deeply about and work closely together to overcome the challenges of communicating information and knowledge across sweeping distances. Sandford Fleming hit upon the idea of standard time to make communications of all kinds more consistent and reliable. Alexander Graham Bell's signature creation set the stage for twentieth-century telephony and the twenty-first-century revolution in global communications. Mike Lazaridis spearheaded creation of the BlackBerry wireless mobile device, generations of which link ever-growing numbers of people throughout the world. And Marshall McLuhan's concept of the global village enabled all the planet's citizens to appreciate the consequences of the new world we're building through our development and use of information and communications technologies. Yet Canada's long-standing desire to be open to the influences and knowledge of the world is reflected most vividly in the human face of our country. We are of many colours, faiths, and backgrounds – as many as the world contains. We are also small in number – some 36 million at last count – spread across a land larger than any except Russia. Any success we have enjoyed as a sparse population living in a vast land is a direct result of our willingness to welcome the world's people, ideas, and knowledge to our shores and to reach out in turn beyond our physical and mental borders.

I've tried to be a knowledge diplomat throughout my career. I started early. I studied at Harvard (as you did at almost the same time) and then at Cambridge as a Rotary Scholar. One of my duties as a scholarship recipient was to visit various chapters of the Rotary Club across Britain and talk about Canada. I continued to reach out across borders and disciplines soon after graduation. One of the first overseas visits I made as a professional was to China. It took place nearly thirty-five years ago – a time when few Canadians or even Westerners had the privilege of experiencing the vibrant life and historic culture of that remarkable land and people. As principal of McGill University, I went there in 1980 just after the Cultural Revolution to restore the Norman Bethune Medical Exchange between McGill and the Peking Medical College. Shortly thereafter we worked with a variety of Chinese professionals to set up a nationwide program in business management education. It was a remarkable success. Our initiative helped more than sixty schools of higher learning in that country develop graduate degree programs in business management. It also spawned forty-seven partnerships between universities in China and Canada. Since then, these programs and partnerships have helped thousands of Chinese men and women get a solid grounding in advanced principles and methods of modern management. This generation of managers has contributed mightily to the unprecedented economic success of China. The collaborations themselves have inspired these and many more schools to reach out across their borders and find many new ways for students, teachers, and researchers from a variety of academic and scientific disciplines to live, study, and work with their peers around the world. They have also enriched the educations of thousands of young Chinese and Canadian men and women, spurred the uncovering of new knowledge in an array of fields, and fostered greater understanding between our two countries.

As you know well, McGill also played a key role in developing your Aga Khan University Hospital in Karachi, Pakistan. You may recall that we first met when it opened in 1981. The McGill team of epidemiology and public health, led by Walter Spitzer (an esteemed McGill epidemiologist), shared its community-medicine model to help the hospital deploy public health services outside the hospital itself. I remember then being struck by how bold your venture was, introducing the best of Western education and health care into a culture with vastly different customs and traditions. One of the most striking of these efforts was to open a school of nursing to educate girls to become nurse practitioners, start these regional clinics, and overcome traditional barriers to women health professionals treating boys and men. I realize now what a supreme exercise in the diplomacy of knowledge it was on the part of your hospital and McGill. You made the model work because you applied it while taking into account those customs and traditions. That's the diplomacy of knowledge truly in action!

I often explain the power of the diplomacy of knowledge across cultures through international education – the healthy diversification of Canadian schools and colleges through the presence of international students and the "awakening" that occurs when young Canadians study, work, or volunteer abroad. I sometimes illustrate this with the personal example of my wife and my five daughters who began their international exchanges at age twelve. Four things happened to them: their natural curiosity – the question *why*, which is on children's lips from when they begin to talk – is piqued. Second, their tolerance, in the best sense of the word, is broadened. They seek out and appreciate difference and they welcome change as a refresher. Third, their judgement is expanded. As the Book of Solomon says, they grow in wisdom and stature. They are slower to jump to conclusions; they look for the whole story; they are quicker to spot bigotry. Or as Saint-Exupéry writes in *Le Petit Prince*, "I am different from you, but because I am different, I don't diminish you; I enhance you." And fourth, something very human. They become more empathetic – not simply feeling the pain of another's discomfort but being able to place themselves in the other person's shoes.

During my time as governor general, I have seen – in dozens of countries on every continent – many other examples of the diplomacy of knowledge in action. Two prime examples of Canadians sharing and refining knowledge with others stand out. The first is the Mulheres Mil Program in Brazil. It involves the Colleges and Institutes Canada and Canada's International Development Research Centre working with the local ministry of education to provide basic education and vocational training to one thousand women. In doing so, the program enables them to enter the labour market, removing them from a position of vulnerability and enhancing the quality of life of themselves, their families, and their communities. After nearly ten years, not only has it achieved its primary goal, but it has also given project directors knowledge to expand the program in Brazil and implement it elsewhere. Another great example is the College of the North Atlantic. The modest Newfoundland-based school won a competition to create a six-thousand-student college of applied arts and sciences in Qatar. The Qataris told me that the College of the North Atlantic was able to beat out some of the world's leading educational institutions because, in their proposal, the Newfoundlanders showed themselves to be resilient, hard-working, and, most importantly, respectful of local conditions. (I like to think that another factor in the Newfoundlanders' favour was the fact that the Qataris didn't want their children speaking English with an Oxbridge accent!)

I have spent a good part of my tenure as Canada's governor general taking insights like these and urging men and women from all walks of life – anthropologists and computer scientists, psychologists and engineers, historians and urban planners, poets and lawyers even – to be knowledge diplomats in their own lives and careers – to reach across borders and disciplines to uncover, test, and establish universal truths, and to spark innovative ideas and practices. I've emphasized the leading role students and teachers can play. I've called on students to choose careers that combine personal success and public service.

And I've asked educators to increase the number of students learning foreign languages; to encourage more of their professors to take their sabbaticals in other countries; to link their research labs with those in other parts of the world; and to arrange accreditation and certification processes to make it possible for students to earn degrees by completing courses and fulfilling requirements at universities in different countries.

My time and travels as governor general make me excited about the future of the diplomacy of knowledge. I've seen how advanced technologies are making communications so quick and easy, and the opportunity to share knowledge ubiquitous and cheap. These twin developments mean ideas are being tested through action more quickly and therefore changes are coming faster than ever before. As ideas are tested and refined, and changes take place, we must be sure to promote and defend the practices that have served us well and also use the diplomacy of knowledge to broaden not only what but how we learn. The good news is, I think, that more and more people understand that the well-being of their countries is defined by how well they develop, share, and advance knowledge. Something you said in your convocation address at the University of Ottawa – that a country's standing in our contemporary world is no longer recognized by what it can achieve for itself but by what it can do for others – leads me to believe we agree on this point. In fact, I'm sure we both speak with one voice when I say everyone must use the beauty and power of the diplomacy of knowledge – as Frank Scott did, as you do – to help secure for all peoples the peace, prosperity, and personal fulfillment that is their birthright and create the smarter, more caring world that is the dream of all humankind.

God bless you.
David

His Highness the Aga Khan is the forty-ninth hereditary leader of the Shia Imami Ismaili Muslims, a role he assumed in 1957, and chairman of the Aga Khan Development Network, one of the world's most successful development organizations. Born in Geneva, he spent his early childhood in Nairobi, Kenya, and then attended Le Rosey School in Switzerland for nine years. He graduated from Harvard University in 1959. Since then, he has received numerous awards, decorations, and honorary degrees in recognition of his work, including honorary citizenship of Canada and companion of the Order of Canada.

Time, Talent, and Treasure

Persuade more Canadians to give.

To Marc Kielburger and Craig Kielburger

Dear Marc and Craig,

All Canadians would give their time, talent, and treasure if they felt the rush of energy, enthusiasm, and excitement I experienced at the National We Day celebration in Ottawa. Your dozen or so We Day gatherings each year across Canada and now in the United States and United Kingdom are spectacular ways to inspire young people in our country and others to give and keep giving. I was thrilled to take advantage of the occasion to present four of these young men and women with the Governor General's Caring Canadian Award – which is now the Sovereign's Medal for Volunteers – for their exceptional achievements in giving. As governor general, I encourage

Canadians of all ages to volunteer and be philanthropists. Volunteerism and philanthropy are essential ingredients in making our country smarter and more caring. And the ways in which we care must be increasingly smarter. National We Day is a perfect example of that intelligence in action – keen minds and kind hearts working together.

The event also got me thinking more deeply than ever about why we give and how we can persuade more Canadians to give. Why do we give? Those who study altruism divide its source into three broad categories: nepotism (altruism is displayed by an individual toward relatives as a means of ensuring the altruist's genes get passed on to another generation); reciprocation (altruism is a business deal between two people based on the premise "I scratch your back, you scratch mine"); and group selection (altruism exists in instances in which the interest of the group trumps that of the individual). The mystery of altruism became especially baffling when Charles Darwin emerged with his findings. The study of altruism suddenly became a question of science and not solely ethics. That question goes basically like this: If all life is a survival of the fittest, then how do we account for the many examples of selflessness in the natural world? Is there such a thing as survival of the nicest? Biologists, psychologists, anthropologists, and neuroscientists took on the challenge with gusto. Three of these thinkers – George Price, William Hamilton, and John Maynard Smith – made the most headway. A breakthrough came when Price applied game theory to the question of altruism and came up with an equation that proved altruism is always – to a lesser or greater degree – a form of disguised self-interest. That's not necessarily a bad thing. As Oren Harman points out in his biography of Price, biology is not destiny; it is capacity. Just as we humans have the capacity for violence and greed, we also have the capacity for kindness and generosity.

I agree. I consider the act of giving an expression of our common humanity – emphasis on *common*. We give to others, with no expectation of receiving anything in return, because we feel a kinship to them. This connection is most powerful among family members. It's also expressed among individuals who belong to the same communities – from tribes and neighbourhoods to cities and countries. In this sense, goodness depends on association and not necessarily on family – the closer the association, the greater the altruism. I especially like the way you put it in your book *Me to We*. You contend that altruism is a key part of the universal human desire to achieve personal fulfillment. We give to others to complete ourselves.

The sense of kinship and community has always been a powerful force for good in Canada. From the first days of human life on this land, volunteers and philanthropists – native-born and newly arrived – have given of themselves and their resources to others freely and selflessly. We can trace that generous ethos of giving from the experiences of Canada's Aboriginal peoples, here before the European settlers. How do we know this to be true? In the first comprehensive history of New France – itself based on the detailed record of Samuel de Champlain – Pierre de Charlevoix observed that Champlain and the other French settlers in Canada learned that the Indians of the St. Lawrence River valley judged the virtue of themselves and other tribes by one fact: how they treated widows, orphans, and the infirm. Inspired by this lesson, the earliest Canadian settlers themselves quickly realized that, if they were going to survive and thrive in this forbidding land, if they were going to build better lives for themselves and their neighbours and hold open brighter futures for their children, they must give freely to others of their time, talent, and treasure. They had to. Like the Aboriginal peoples of this land, they realized that our country is too vast, our climate too harsh, the challenges of starting anew too daunting for anyone – even the strongest and most resourceful – to make it on their own. Evidence of these challenges and of the generosity of the Indians was clear at Champlain's first settlement at Port Royal in 1608: Indians shared fresh meat with the settlers and also taught them how to make a tea from spruce needles, which prevented scurvy.

The experiences of those early Canadians lit a spark that soon grew into a bright flame. Merchants in New France set up the Office of the Poor. The first voluntary agency in Canada, it found work for the unemployed; gave food, money, and shelter to the sick, elderly, and incapacitated; and supplied tools to labourers so they could carry out their trades. Other organizations soon followed. Local parishes, religious orders, and lay groups founded charities such as the Hall of God, the House of Providence, and the Society of Saint Vincent de Paul to support the destitute, care for the sick and elderly, and teach young boys and girls from poor families. In the decades following

Confederation, volunteer groups sprang up across Canada to help settle European immigrants and keep their traditional cultures alive: immigrants from Iceland set up a network of libraries and reading clubs; Canadians of German birth in Halifax established the country's first funeral and burial society; Canadians from Poland who settled in Kitchener founded Canada's first mutual-aid society; and homesteaders from Hungary and Ukraine became unofficial settling agents, helping newcomers from all lands start new lives on the vast Canadian prairie. As our country grew, crusading advocates such as the St. John Ambulance Association, Canadian Red Cross Society, and Young Women's Christian Association provided crucial services to vulnerable people such as children and young women, and spearheaded social reform to help ensure all Canadians had access to decent homes, adequate health care, and free education. In recent years, dozens of community groups such as the United Way, Habitat for Humanity, and the Community Foundations of Canada have been formed to respond to community needs, economic hardship, natural disasters, and war. National charitable organizations such as the Canadian Lung Association, Canadian Cystic Fibrosis Foundation, Muscular Dystrophy Canada, Alzheimer Society of Canada, and many others have raised hundreds of billions of dollars to help find cures for diseases and help comfort those afflicted with them. At the same time, development agencies based in our country are taking the conviction, passion, and know-how of Canadians and applying them to help people throughout the world – your Free the Children being a standout.

The spirit of giving runs like a vivid thread through the fabric of our country's history. Most Canadians can call on telling examples. My family lived in an Ontario farming community for many years and we saw that spirit alive and well in the tradition of Mennonite barn-raisings, where a community rallies to help whenever a farming family – of any faith – must build or repair a building.

One of the ways in which our family has responded over the years was through education. My wife, Sharon, and I felt strongly that we wanted to honour Sharon's mother and grandmother, two women who meant much to us. Both women were single mothers who raised families and, despite the challenges, provided good lives for their children. When I worked at the University of Waterloo, we seized the chance to honour their memory. We set up a bursary fund for women doing graduate studies who had overcome their own hardships. What a rewarding experience that has been! To this day, we get letters from the women who were awarded these bursaries. They have accomplished much and are thankful for the opportunities they've had. To know we played a small part in helping them succeed is a wonderful feeling. We achieve personal fulfillment by giving to others. It's our giving moment, and it's one that keeps on giving – to those women and to Sharon and me.

What have I learned from my experience and, more so, from our country's long and shared history of giving? I've learned that giving has evolved from being an activity carried out by a select few to a mass activity in which every person can contribute because everyone has something of value to offer. I've learned that new Canadians have brought to our shores new ways of thinking about giving. And I've learned that the very idea of giving is never static. Thousands of Canadians right now are serving their communities in ways that neither they nor others would likely define as giving in the traditional sense. Though this work exists outside of conventional bounds, it's of great value because it encourages others to contribute in unconventional ways and it helps all of us form a truer idea of citizenship. Why have Canadians in communities across our country embraced this kind of giving so closely? It's because while volunteering most often takes place in our neighbourhoods, we know that when we combine our volunteer efforts with others, we do more than help and support those locally. We nourish our shared country, making it stronger, healthier, and more vibrant for us all. We create a healthy nation that is the sum of the individual healthy communities that make it up. That's why there are few tasks more noble or profound or personally fulfilling and collectively meaningful than the seemingly simple act of helping, sharing, giving. There are some who say people give their time, talent, and treasure solely because of what they themselves get out of it. Go for it, I say. If your sole motivation to give is in order to receive, then give and keep giving. Let's have more of that kind of satisfaction and that kind of selfishness and together we'll build a pretty attractive world.

Yet recent research carried out in the United States shows that the science behind giving is more complex and astonishing than we've ever conceived. Mike Norton, a professor at Harvard Business School, has conducted research that suggests money above a certain modest sum does not have the power to buy happiness, and yet even very rich people continue to believe that it does. Norton uncovered one exception to this rule: while spending money on oneself does nothing for one's happiness, spending it on others increases that happiness. Other researchers are finding that excessive wealth actually influences the behaviour of the wealthy. Keely Muscatell, a UCLA neuroscientist, has published a paper that shows wealth quiets the nerves in the brain associated with empathy. She says that, as a person becomes wealthier and moves up the class ladder, the more likely that person is to lie, cheat, shoplift, violate the rules of the road, and be tight-fisted when it comes to giving to others. Michael Lewis, the writer and polymath, concludes that this research shows that wealth "tilts" the brains of the privileged, "causing them to be less likely to care about anyone but themselves or to experience the moral sentiments needed to be a decent citizen." Findings of University of British Columbia researcher John Helliwell shed an even brighter light on this phenomenon: we derive greater satisfaction and happiness from the number, richness, and diversity of our social connections than we do from the size of our bank accounts. We are much happier when we give generously of ourselves than we are when we accumulate and keep for ourselves alone.

These truly incredible findings bring me to my next question: How we can persuade more Canadians to give? To answer that question, I think we have to recognize that giving is somewhat different today. Until now, giving has been largely people responding to pressing, immediate needs. Today – and more into the future – giving is as much about finding ways to help that were never even dreamed of a generation ago. Retired workers are rechannelling their hard-won professional knowledge, skills, and experiences to teach and help others. New Canadians are enabling all Canadians to take advantage of different traditions of helping. And Canadians of all backgrounds and ages are going online and using advanced communications technologies to carry out virtual volunteering, micro-volunteering, customer volunteering, on-demand volunteering, and crowd-sourcing. As you know very well, young Canadians are especially goal-oriented, mobile, and tech-savvy. They set aside conventional methods and use new technologies to find exciting ways to express their willingness to help – whether it's accessing Facebook to help identify missing people in the aftermath of the Haitian earthquake; taking advantage of their tech skills to build websites for charitable organizations in developing countries; or making the most of their smartphones to conduct quick bursts of volunteer activity several times throughout the course of a day. In these and many other ways, young Canadians are changing the very nature of giving.

As the world becomes more complex, we need to continually reinvent how giving works. We need especially to be more sensitive to changing needs, to find new ways of delivering help, and, particularly in a society such as ours that believes so much in equality of opportunity, to ensure we don't have nearly so many gaps in where our giving goes. Our Aboriginal communities are for the most part in a very difficult position, and that's something that should alarm us. We also have an increasing gap of skills that's contributing to an economy in which there are people without jobs and jobs without people. And as society shifts and the role of government changes, we need to encourage individuals and governments to join forces to achieve shared goals. Mike Lazaridis's actions are a great example of this kind of collaboration. He invested some $300 million of his own money in an institute for theoretical physics (for theory) and an institute for quantum computing (for experimentation). He has captured the imagination of governments to see that Canada has an opportunity to be a leader in quantum mechanics. That's a brilliant private-public partnership that started with a philanthropic gift but that will build a whole new industry. By reinventing how giving works, we can ensure all Canadians give of their time, talent, and treasure. In the reinventing, we must make giving not a switch Canadians turn on when something catches their attention and then off when their attention drifts to something else. We should make giving intrinsic and innate so that we give simply because it's established behaviour. What are we going to do as a country and as Canadians to make sure the on-off switch of giving is always on? Three ideas come to mind:

We must make giving as uncomplicated as possible. Just as governments try to create regulatory environments in which new businesses have few barriers to entry, we must make sure Canadians have no barriers to giving. No complicated processes; no complex procedures; no convoluted practices. Giving in all its forms should be as easy as dropping a coin into an empty cup.

We must identify and stress the qualities we share as a means of encouraging greater giving. Since relatedness has proven to be the sturdiest predictor of altruistic behaviour, we must convincingly expand our definition of community to encompass as many people as possible.

We must open up ever more avenues for people – especially young people – to give their time, talent, and treasure, as well as new methods to show our appreciation as a country to those who give. As you have shown, the greatest act of giving is to encourage others to give. I call it *widening the circle of giving.* I've travelled across our country to meet with Canada's top philanthropists – especially those from the business world – to urge them to mentor and nurture the next generation of Canadian philanthropists. Your National We Day is a great way to widen the circle of giving by spurring young people to find their own ways to give. Who knows how many boys and girls and young men and women have been and will be inspired not only by your example, but also by your encouragement and the confidence you show them?

At Rideau Hall we try to make giving uncomplicated, inclusive, and expansive. We re-launched the Caring Canadian Award as a way to acknowledge outstanding volunteers who give of their time and talent to help others. My Giving Moment is an effort in which we teamed up with leading corporate, community, and media organizations to encourage Canadians to give to their neighbours, communities, charities, and causes. And Dare2Give – which is a component of My Giving Moment – gives Canadians an opportunity to dare their friends, family, and colleagues to donate or volunteer with them. Research shows that one of the main reasons people give is simply because someone asks them; an effective way to ask someone to do something is to dare them – in person, on-line, and across social media. This finding corresponds with the fascinating new research I mentioned earlier. Even those disinclined to give can be compelled to do so if they are encouraged clearly and frequently. As Michael Lewis points out, many of the wealthiest and most privileged among us possess the self-awareness to correct for whatever tricks brain chemicals seek to play on them. They just need to be reminded to give – loudly and often. This point reinforces what Oren Harman said in his Price biography: our biology is not our destiny. We have a choice. All of us can be givers.

You two young Canadian leaders have made the choice to give and to encourage others to give – clearly and frequently. I can think of nothing that is smarter and more caring than that.

Your friend,
David

Marc Kielburger and Craig Kielburger are co-founders of Free the Children and Me to We, co-hosts of National We Day. At twenty-eight and twenty-five years of age respectively, they are among the youngest individuals to be invested into the Order of Canada. Free the Children is active in dozens of countries, building schools and educating children. Me to We is a for-profit social enterprise that sells socially responsible products and services and donates half its profits to Free the Children. National We Day is an annual gathering of thousands of young people in Ottawa, the nation's capital. This event, like others in the country and beyond, is meant to spur young men and women to fulfill their potential as active citizens.

The New, Noisy Word

Why Canadians should shout about innovation.

To Kevin Lynch

Dear Kevin,

I always have time for people who are candid with cause, and I've been meaning to tell you for some time now how arrested I was by your recent warning that Canadian businesses have not been motivated to invest in innovation because the Canadian dollar has been so strong.

As I write, our dollar is about as weak as it's been in decades, so that has to change.

Let's start by defining terms. Certain words have appeal in certain times. Terms such as *prudence* and *temperance*, while no longer in their heyday, have enjoyed great currency in other times. In ours, *innovation* has only recently appeared in common use. Although its use may recede in future decades, it is of profound importance today. One can find it in countless business proposals, government policies, and, tellingly, media stories. That's some relief.

I appreciated the way you defined innovation simply as "anytime you change a product or service and get value back." I assume by *value* you mean anything with perceivable (at least) and measurable (at best) merit to any particular beneficiary. Let's look at that. While my own career may be seen by some to have been predominantly academic, administrative, and, lately, diplomatic, I have deep conviction that every economy prospers only when entrepreneurs have the gumption to build products and services that people actually need. The fact that those needs change over time requires that product makers and service providers keep thinking of new things to build and offer – things that customers will see as truly valuable.

What helps make that possible on a national level? On one hand, it is a cultural ethos supported by public policy. You no doubt know of the book *Everything I Needed to Know About Business . . . I Learned from a Canadian*. In it, Leonard Brody and David Raffa propose that a key advantage enjoyed by Canadian innovators has been their access to health care that follows them wherever they go in Canada. Without having to worry about losing their health benefits, innovative Canadians can hop from region to region, company to company, employer to employer, following opportunities to do their best work. With our most inventive souls able to up stakes whenever opportunity presents itself, the result has been a kind of contagion of innovation where innovative thinking meets innovative design meets innovative manufacturing meets innovative marketing more often than not. Incubators of business in more than one nearby nation have looked at that advantage with some envy, the authors tell us.

I believe that observation is as valid today as it ever was, but we're missing some of the excitement that inspires great people to do new things. We've known for some time that we've needed a national innovation award program here in Canada. I was deeply happy to be able to launch one under the banner of the Governor General's Innovation Awards. I believe that Canadians are some of the world's most accomplished innovators, yet we seldom recognize ourselves as such or celebrate our outstanding contributions to our society and to humanity as a whole. By recognizing our great innovators, including those of the next generation and those who promote social innovation, we hope to strengthen the culture of innovation that is crucial to our nation.

Ceremonies honouring our innovators are, I hope you'll agree, one part of what must be a nation-wide solution. There is no doubt in my mind that bringing public attention to the finest examples of Canadian innovation will have an impact on the public mind.

Words like *temperance* and *prudence* may be only quietly spoken these days. Let's make sure *innovation* is as noisy a word as it can be.

Appreciatively,
David

The Honourable Kevin Lynch is a Cape Breton–born economist with a celebrated career in both business and government. From 2006 to 2009, he served as Clerk of the Privy Council – the top federal post in Canada's public service. Today he is vice-chair of the BMO Financial Group, past chair of the Board of Governors of the University of Waterloo, and chancellor of University of King's College in Halifax. His comments regarding innovation, which Mr. Johnston alludes to, were made before the Canadian Club.

Part Three

What Inspires Me

Soul of Our Nation

In gratitude for sacrifice.

To the Unknown Soldier

Son,

At the eleventh hour on the eleventh day of the eleventh month, when the guns of the Great War at last fell silent, the fury of conflict was replaced by a deafening silence. In that fragile gap between the sounds of massacre and the cries of relief, we were faced with all we had done, all we had lost, all we had sacrificed. In that silence, we met a truth so obvious and so terrifying we swore we would never take up arms again. "One owes respect to the living," said Voltaire. "To the dead, one owes only the truth."

We vowed never to forget. We built monuments – massive pillars of stone and metal – and placed them at the very heart of our towns and cities, so they might stop us daily in our tracks. We collected names, wrote these names in books, and carved them into walls in our anguished effort to save those we failed from the damnation of anonymity. And we pledged to gather in our communities each year at this hour on this singular day of Remembrance so that we might fall silent again . . . and again . . . and again.

Each year – on that day, at that hour – many thousands stand as one in silent tribute to them at our National War Memorial, a monument that King George VI called "the spontaneous response of the nation's conscience, revealing the very soul of the nation."

When I invite people to visit our memorial, I urge them to look upward and against the sky see the bronze figures of Peace and Freedom. Their arms are linked. They cannot be separated. Because freedom without peace is agony, and peace without freedom is slavery, and we will tolerate neither. This is the truth we owe our dead.

Then I urge them to look down, to your own resting place. We don't know your name. You are our unknown soldier. In anonymity, you honour all Canadians who died and may yet die for their country. Sadly, Nathan Cirillo and Patrice Vincent are now among them. We stand on guard for you and for them.

We are people of peace. Of respect and tolerance, kindness and honour. These qualities are alive in our national conscience precisely because we hold them as precious. We have the luxury to do so because those we remember believed those qualities to be precious enough to die for. That is why we will keep those men and women in our memory for all time. "Without memory," said Rabbi Dow Marmur, "there can be neither continuity nor identity."

We have had sombre occasion to ponder our identity as this very symbol of our peace and freedom was mocked and violated on an October day not long ago. Yet here at your side we continue to stand, and here we shall remain: unshaken in resolve; grateful in remembrance of those who have sacrificed; dedicated, like the memorial, to our eternal duty: peace and freedom – the very soul of our nation.

In gratitude,
David

The Canadian Tomb of the Unknown Soldier lies in the shadow of the National War Memorial in Confederation Square, Ottawa. The tomb holds the remains of an unidentified Canadian soldier who fell near Vimy Ridge, the site of a fierce battle in France in 1917 that still holds deep symbolic value for Canadians. Corporal Nathan Frank Cirillo was a twenty-four-year-old reservist with the Argyll and Sutherland Highlanders of Canada who, while standing sentry over the tomb on October 22, 2014, was wounded by a gunman and subsequently died. Warrant Officer Patrice Vincent had been killed two days earlier when an assailant deliberately drove his vehicle into Vincent and another member of the Canadian Armed Forces as a premeditated act of terrorism.

Solving a Mystery. Building a Nation.

Why Charlevoix makes me proud of the whole country.

To Richard and Sylvia Cruess

Dear Richard and Sylvia,

Much of what Sharon and I know about the history of medicine in Canada springs from our friendship with you both. I was reminded of our early conversations just weeks ago, when once again we found a quiet day or two to visit Charlevoix.

As I've grown ever so slightly older (just recently, of course), I've come to the conclusion that secret hideaways are a great source of comfort. For me, Charlevoix is one of these ideal spots. Nestled against the northern shore of the St. Lawrence about an hour's drive from Quebec, this exquisite region has about everything a Canadian could want in a getaway – a restorative combination of nature and culture that reawakens the spirit and makes one proud of the whole country at the same time.

How many other places can say that their relevant history goes back 350 million years? In Charlevoix, nine out of ten residents live in a crater formed when a meteor two kilometres across weighing 15 billion tonnes slammed into the surface. That meteor created one of the twelve largest craters on our planet, flattening a vast area of the Laurentians that, after a few ice ages, is now an expanse of rolling fields nestled among gentle hills.

Les Éboulements (literally *the landslides* and one of the province's most scenic villages) lies at the heart of it all, and if you're there and you daydream you might think you're in the Yorkshire Dales.

You both know how much I love this spot, as do you. Dotted with pleasant farmlands, idyllic villages, and tiny municipalities to which tourists rightly flock, Charlevoix takes in a considerable portion of both the Grand Jardin National Park and the Laurentides Wildlife Preserve – an amazing stretch of unspoiled land that totals 7,800 square kilometres of lakes (two thousand of them) and rivers (nine of them) in which Canadian wildlife proliferates. And in this vast expanse of perfect natural splendour, the human population is zero. Zero.

And despite (or perhaps in addition to) the staggering natural beauty of the place, there is one historic moment that inspires me. I'm sure you know it well – a moment in history that I take as early evidence of the public spirit that has shaped health care in Canada into the present day. Back in 1757, the French surgeon Philippe-Louis-François Badelard came to Louisbourg and two years later fetched up in Quebec at the Plains of Abraham. Not long after, he was captured by the British. Badelard had talent and a considerable reputation for his expertise. Highly skilled in the arts of medicine and therefore highly valued by all, he was quickly returned to service, this time as surgeon to the Canadian militia, with whom in 1775 he helped defend Quebec against American forces under Benedict Arnold. His talents were too valuable to squander – a classic example of the diplomacy of knowledge at work.

In 1776, Governor Guy Carleton approached Badelard and implored him to turn those talents to solving a medical mystery that had been puzzling residents of Charlevoix for two years. A hitherto unknown disease was wreaking havoc in the region. For anyone unfortunate enough to contract the ailment (at its height claiming 5 per cent of the population), what began as a sore throat would quickly progress to agonizing joint pain and ulceration of the genitals, and end with wholesale disintegration of the victim's bone tissue. Horrific. No one could figure out what was at play. The only shred of evidence was that the malady appeared not long after the arrival of Scottish soldiers in the area.

Badelard made the mystery his central focus from 1776 to 1784. He named the infirmity *le mal de la baie St-Paul* and travelled from parish to parish treating its victims and looking for its source. He cracked it, of course. It was an unseen strain of venereal disease brought by the Scots. His curative treatments ranged from a light diet with greatly reduced consumption of meat to the ingestion of mercury, which seemed to work despite the resulting loss of teeth!

Yet that's not the best part. What appeals to me is the way Badelard and Carleton went at the project. Alarmed that one in twenty residents were being felled by the disease, the doctor and the governor agreed that all patients should be given immediate medical treatment – without judgement and without cost.

I often amuse myself by reflecting on the genesis of those institutions that make Canada unique. Here in Charlevoix in the late eighteenth century we have one of the earliest examples of Canadian universal health care – available to all at no direct cost to the patient. That the decision to handle the issue in this novel way sprang from collaboration between a French medical expert and an English administrator makes me proud. It is yet another of the countless proofs that the genesis of our unique culture here in Canada is the fortuitous and unbeatable combination of Anglo and French instincts.

Any Canadian visiting the region would do well to reflect on that story. Especially when sampling the cider on Isle aux Coudres or the Migneron cheese (preferably baked) in Baie-Saint-Paul.

Warmly,
David

David and Sharon Johnston are long-time friends of Richard and Sylvia Cruess. Dr. Richard Leigh Cruess, a companion of the Order of Canada, is a Canadian orthopaedic surgeon and academic who served as dean of the McGill University Faculty of Medicine from 1981 to 1995, during which time Mr. Johnston was principal. Dr. Cruess co-authored the fascinating *Brief History of Medicine at McGill*. Dr. Sylvia Cruess, a member of the Order of Canada, is an endocrinologist and was medical director of the Royal Victoria Hospital (1978–1995). Since their "retirement," they have embarked on a new joint career as scholars on the redefinition of professionalism in the health disciplines and are amongst the most respected international leaders in this challenging field. All four friends share a love of Canadian history. And cheese.

It Dares Us

Our flag challenges Canadians anew.

To George Stanley

Dear George,

Did you ever in your wildest dreams think, way back in 1965, our country's flag would become such a beloved and universally recognized symbol of Canada and Canadians?

My guess is you thought then that we had made an excellent decision to have our own flag and an equally excellent decision to choose your design. Yet I suspect you had no inkling our flag – the Stanley flag – would be embraced so warmly by Canadians. That red maple leaf between red bars is now so embedded in our national life, so emblematic of our national purpose, we simply cannot imagine our country without it. It stands for the people we are, the values we cherish, and the land we call home – from Atlantic to Pacific to the very top of the world.

Not too shabby a feat for a historian. Although you were a historian by training and profession, you were a master designer by instinct: your single maple leaf design has the virtue of simplicity; it also emphasizes a distinctive Canadian symbol; and it suggests the idea of loyalty to a single country. Unlike many amateur designers in the sixties, you believed wisely that a new Canadian flag must avoid any symbols associated with other countries, such as the Union Jack and Fleur de Lys. Our flag must be just that – our flag and ours alone.

Millions of Canadians agreed with you then. Thousands of them gathered on Parliament Hill on February 15, 1965, to watch as our new flag was hoisted high and flew for the first time in the skies over Canada. Governor General Georges Vanier was one of them. Your friend John Matheson called the mere presence of the dignified Vanier a benediction. As the frigid February winds whipped across the red maple leaf, Monsieur Vanier called that new flag "a symbol of the unity of purpose and high resolve to which destiny beckoned all Canadians."

What that day and those words and, most of all, that flag represented was then – and remains now – unmistakable. Together, they symbolized an increasingly hopeful Canada. From that day on, we would think bigger and reach further than ever before. They also symbolized a rapidly emergent Canada. From that day on, we would define ourselves less through the prism of our past and more by the promise of our future.

Our new flag would be central to that future. Neither forged in the fire of war nor raised at the ramparts of revolution, it represented the country Canada was striving to become, and it dared Canadians to achieve that becoming. It dared Canadians to be just as bold as that new flag, just as colourful, spirited, and vibrant. It dared Canadians to build a country worthy of that flag: a country that is smart and caring, peaceful and prosperous, inclusive and fair; a country that strides continually closer to justice, equality, and excellence. We were ready for that new flag and, at the same time, we needed it to spur us on.

That same flag flies proudly over the nation we have become – the country those Canadians dreamed of and determined to build long ago. Our flag has not aged since that day in 1965. It never frays, never fades. It remains as vivid and vital today as it did when the winds over the Peace Tower first took hold and unfurled it for all the world to see.

And just as our flag dared Canadians then, I think you will be happy and gratified to know it calls to Canadians of this day. Our flag dares us to press on with the unfinished work of our country: to be ever more free and fair, just and inclusive; to be keener of mind and kinder of heart. Though we may speak different languages, practise different faiths, or originate from different corners of the globe, our flag dares all Canadians to be forever united and willing to live and build together, and in doing so be an inspiration and guide to people throughout the world and to generations unborn here at home.

Just as Canadians responded to Governor General Vanier and his call to realize the unity of purpose and high resolve to which destiny has summoned Canada, I know Canadians in the years to come will embrace our very own challenge and fulfill the promise of our country once again. Amazing what the right flag – your flag, our flag – can do.

With deepest thanks,
David

George F.G. Stanley (1907–2002) is widely recognized as the designer of Canada's flag. In 1964, he wrote a detailed letter to John Matheson – a prominent member of a parliamentary committee charged with identifying and recommending a new flag – in which Stanley outlined his design and the rationale behind it. A Rhodes Scholar at the University of Oxford, he wrote several definitive volumes on Louis Riel and the Riel Rebellions, taught history at several universities, including Royal Military College for twenty years, and was founding director of the Canadian studies program at Mount Allison University, the first program of its kind. A companion of the Order of Canada, Stanley ended his teaching career in 1975 but remained active in public life, serving as lieutenant governor of New Brunswick from 1981 to 1987.

Nation of Losers

How the world's poor built a winning country.

To Lin Su

Dear Su,

Canada is a nation of losers. Are you shocked to hear that? You've just become a citizen of Canada and here I am – someone who was born here and lived most of my life here – telling you that your new home is a collection of washouts! Now that I have your attention, allow me to explain what I mean. Hugh MacLennan, one of our country's great novelists, came up with that phrase. (You should read his novels. Every Canadian should. His stories and characters give a powerful sense of who we are as a people. His most famous is *Two Solitudes*, but I have a soft spot for his last novel, *Voices in Time*.)

MacLennan was being playful and provocative when he wrote those words. He didn't mean them in a demeaning or disrespectful sense. He meant that generations of Canadians came to this country from abroad to take hold of the opportunities available to them here and make better lives for themselves and for their families. They included Americans who were loyal to the British Crown and thus were persona non grata in the new republic; Scots who left a land where, for a time, sheep were considered more valuable than people; Irish starved out of their homeland as a result of the potato famine; Eastern Europeans and Russians who fled political and religious persecution; Western Europeans who sought better lives in the aftermath of the most destructive war in human history; people from Asia, Africa, and the Middle East who escaped violence and poverty. Over many centuries, these so-called losers who came with nothing more than a fierce determination that life should be better for their children – together with their native-born compatriots – built a very special country.

How were so many able to succeed here in Canada when they met with mostly disappointment and defeat in their countries of birth? Inclusiveness. This country is an economically prosperous and socially cohesive country because we Canadians have built political and economic institutions that are inclusive. Inclusive economic institutions are the right to hold private property; an unbiased system of law that enforces contracts; public services that create a level playing field on which people can exchange and contract freely and fairly; and commercial and labour markets that enable new businesses to enter and compete with others, and make it possible for all people to choose their careers. Inclusive political institutions are those that allow power to be distributed broadly in society and that constrain the powerful from exercising their authority arbitrarily or undermining the foundations of inclusive institutions. They are also institutions that have created public education systems that are accessible, affordable, and of high quality, which more than anything else show that these societies cherish equality of opportunity and excellence, too. Countries fail when their political and economic institutions become extractive. Extractive institutions concentrate political power and economic opportunity in the hands of a few select people or groups and thereby make not only poverty endemic, but also famines, epidemics, civil wars, and mass displacements of people more likely. History is replete with examples of ancient societies and modern nations that have failed – or are failing – because of their extractive politics and economies. Think only of North and South Korea over the past sixty years to see an example of both sides of this coin.

My views on the value of inclusive institutions and the destructive influence of extractive ones are informed by and reflected in a book called *Why Nations Fail.* It's the work of Massachusetts Institute of Technology economist Daron Acemoglu and Harvard University political scientist James Robinson, and is another book I recommend you read. It's a product of the interdisciplinary research on complex world problems led by an extraordinary Canadian innovation – the Canadian Institute for Advanced Research.

The acronym – CIFAR – communicates its ambition when you say it out loud with a soft C. The authors' perspective runs counter to flawed views about growth and development based on determinants such as culture, geography, and ignorance. When we approach the success or failure of societies and countries from the perspective of inclusiveness, we go a long way toward uncovering answers to pressing questions about the fates of countries throughout the world: Is China's rapid economic expansion at odds with its authoritarian government? Is the broadening gulf between rich and poor in the United States sustainable? Is increasing amounts of money transferred from developed countries the most effective way for the world's poorest nations to rise from crushing poverty?

We can also use this perspective to understand precisely why we in Canada have been so successful. All Canadians can access quality health care services regardless of where they live and their ability to pay. Women enjoy the same rights and are able to take advantage of the same opportunities as men (although there is always more that can be done). Most young people in our country can get a quality education regardless of their income, religion, and class. These aspects of inclusion unleash, empower, and protect the full potential of each citizen – man or woman, young or old, immigrant or native-born – to develop in his or her own way. Inclusiveness is not assimilation or even perfect equality. It does not make us all the same. It frees each and every one of us to be exactly who we wish to be – if we work hard enough, study long enough, dream big enough. Canada is far from perfect. Yet our country is a glowing example of what kind of country people can build when the institutions they create are designed to enable our country's citizens to reach their full potential, experience the fullest degree of freedom, and enjoy lives that are rewarding, fulfilling, and meaningful.

As a student, teacher, and university executive, I've seen and experienced the power of quality public education in particular to transform lives and enrich our country. Most of the successes I've enjoyed in my life spring directly from the high-quality education that I received. Public education is a direct product of Canada's inclusive political and economic institutions and is a key engine in our country's prosperity. The great thing about Canadian education is how inclusive it is – from kindergarten to post-secondary school. We as Canadians – and our ancestors for generations before us – made a deliberate choice. We chose not to use education to perpetuate elite groups or a ruling class. We believe we make all our citizens stronger by holding open opportunities – especially opportunities to learn – as widely as possible, and we expand to the full the talent base from which the nation can draw.

I talk about inclusiveness and the political and economic institutions that actively encourage it when I meet with foreign leaders here in Canada and while travelling around the world. I talk with presidents, prime ministers, and ambassadors about what they can learn from Canada's experience and vice versa. My conversation with German chancellor Angela Merkel stands out. During her visit to Canada in 2012, we met and talked about both our countries' efforts to become more inclusive. The conversation began with her question "How do you make this crazy quilt of diversity work in Canada?" She pointed out that Germany's current leaders had learned much from Canada, especially the steps we take to make sure newcomers can reach their full potential and thereby make meaningful contributions for the benefit of all in our country.

I was heartened by her observations. I also took it as a challenge. We Canadians must do an even better job to reward innovation in all aspects of life; to create new incentives for people to contribute to their country; to expand the educational, career, and business choices open to people; to make our governments and public institutions more accessible, responsive, and accountable to the people they serve. It is a challenge I pass on to you and ask you to fulfill as well. I ask you to embrace the inclusive nature of your new home. Take advantage of the opportunities that are available to you to reach your full human potential, and do everything you can to make sure these opportunities and more are available to today's Canadians and those to come. While we cannot create a perfect future for ourselves and our country, we can influence and enhance that future by pushing ourselves and our country in a particular direction. For us in Canada, that influencing process means making our institutions more inclusive.

That's what I ask of you. Oh, and one last thing: Welcome to the nation of losers!

Inclusively yours,
David

Lin Su is the altered name of a woman who has just become a citizen of Canada. She represents all the men and women who will soon become Canadian citizens. She was selected for two reasons. First, China is today the source of more immigrants to Canada than any other country. When translated to English, Lin Su means beautiful forest – a perfectly fitting name for one of the newest Canadians. Second, the Johnston family sponsored a young woman to come from China to Canada to further her education. She earned a Master of Education degree at McGill University and a Master of Business Administration at Concordia University. She then started her own translation business in Montreal, becoming an outstanding language teacher. She was a close friend of the Johnstons' second daughter, Alex, who held a scholarship to learn Mandarin at the Beijing Language Institute in the Chinese capital. This young woman was one of Alex's teachers, who as a result of this association decided she wanted to come to Canada.

Remember the Name

Why French culture is one of Canada's greatest assets.

To Céline Dion

Dear Céline,

Since we met last year at La Citadelle in Quebec, one of the two official residences of the governor general, I've had something on my mind that I'd like to voice now. Let me put my thoughts in context by stating first that I am floored by what you have accomplished – for yourself, your family, your province, your country, your fellow performers and artists around the world, and your almost unfathomable number of loyal fans.

Your confidence in and devotion to your art from the day you were born was well founded in that your natural talent is almost extra-human. Your voice dances, stomps, drifts, drives, flits, and soars across five octaves, at once graceful and almost frighteningly powerful with the ability, as Chuck Taylor once put it, "to render emotion that shakes the soul."

Your voice has left people speechless since your youngest days. (Some, I've heard, have even mortgaged their houses to hear more of it.) More than 200 million have bought your albums, and one can hardly imagine how many times those records and CDs have been loaned to others. Quite frankly, you are one of the best-known voices in musical history. It was no idle boast when your self-titled album declared on its cover, "Remember the name, because you'll never forget the voice." We haven't.

You are an international phenomenon and an artist who has never forgotten her roots – back in Charlemagne and within the vibrant and proud French Canadian culture from which you spring. I recall your publicly refusing to accept a Félix award in 1991 as English Artist of the Year – reminding all of us that no matter which language you perform in, you will always be a French artist. That remarkable declaration has proved to be a simple fact, given your subsequent recording in what must be a dozen other languages – Latin, Mandarin, and Japanese among them.

Any doubts as to your identity were removed forever with *D'Eux*, an album known in the United States simply as "the French album." The twentieth album of your career, it was already your seventeenth in French. So perfectly in tune with your culture as a *Québécoise* and francophone, it's no wonder that *D'Eux* became the all-time best-selling album in France . . . ever.

Céline, your pride of heritage is part of the reason I'm writing. During the many happy years our family lived in Montreal, I saw that kind of pride alive and strong in every quarter of French Canadian culture. Nothing new of course. French culture in Canada has been vibrant since the first visits in the earliest days of contact with our Aboriginal hosts in this land. Mark Lescarbot was writing plays for performance here for audiences of both French and Mi'kmaq more than three hundred years before Michel Tremblay and Robert LePage (his worthy successors) were even born.

Playwrights, poets, and raconteurs have been spinning yarns in French Canada from the beginning. There are more folktales in French Canadian culture than in any other in the Americas (other than those of the Aboriginal peoples) combined, in part because the inventive artists of New France borrowed tales from French, English, Celtic, and native traditions and wove them into a distinct new canon – a sort of folkloric dubstep mix-tape with a *habitant* flair. And within everything, there was a twinkle of humour. When we were living in Quebec, *Juste Pour Rire* in Montreal and *Grand Rire* down in Quebec were becoming huge hits. This comedic tradition with its accent on gentle teasing is also rooted deeply in local culture. I know from my reading that as early as 1565, pranksters made fun of their friends by surreptitiously pinning fish on the backs of their unsuspecting friends' jackets. And that's just the first recorded instance; those guys were probably pinning seafood on each other on the way over from France. Ah, *les poissons d'Avril.*

Look at what's happened to film in Quebec since the 1960s, when young creatives could sharpen their skills through ambitious National Film Board programs designed to promote regional filmmaking. *Mon Oncle Antoine* – now over forty years old – is still thought by many critics to be the best and most influential Canadian film ever to hit the screen. Of late, the incredible talents of the likes of Denis Villeneuve (*Incendies*), Philippe Falardeau (*Monsieur Lazhar*), and Kim Nguyen (*War Witch*) have earned Oscar nominations – just a few of the vast number of honours heaped on the products of French Canadian cinema.

As I have a deep fondness for literature (my grandchildren call me Grampa Book), I'll end by declaring my bottomless enthusiasm for French Canadian literature. Not surprising to me, the first novel written in Quebec (Philippe Aubert de Gaspé's *Le chercheur de trésors*) was commonly known as *L'influence d'un livre.* Since then, the influence of French Canadian books on Canadian art, theatre, cinema, music, politics, and culture in general has been immense. Names like Gabrielle Roy, Marie-Claire Blais, Anne Hébert, Roch Carrier, Mavis Gallant, Émile Nelligan – while just a tiny handful – stand with their Quebec colleagues as among the best writers the world has produced. Even in translation, their work has a power, depth, and reach that, like all great fiction, takes a bewitching hold on the reader. Let's call it charm. (I can still see in my mind's eye every house on Rue Deschambault.)

And so, Céline, as a charmer yourself, I know you will understand my conviction that French Canadian culture as expressed through its arts is one of the great features of Canadian intellectual, aesthetic, and social life. What a dull group we would be without it.

Thank you for having given your entire career to the noble purpose of sharing the culture that you so proudly affirmed back in 1991. No, you are not an English artist. You are a French artist. And without question, you are a great Canadian artist and an artist of the world. So too is your culture not English culture but French, and certainly Canadian, and clearly one of the great cultures of the world.

Thank you for helping me understand that, Céline.
David

Céline Dion is one of the most prolific and successful musical talents of her age and the female artist credited with more record sales and performance income than any of her peers. Mr. Johnston met Céline in 2014 in Quebec when she was honoured yet again with the Order of Canada, this time with elevation to the rank of companion for "a lifetime of outstanding achievement and merit of the highest degree, especially in service to Canada or to humanity at large."

Ask Only to Serve

The highest of callings.

To Canadians born in the twenty-first century

Dear Canadians born in the twenty-first century,

Service. That was the first word I spoke upon becoming governor general of Canada. I chose to utter that word before all others because I believe service is the most important quality any person can hold and express. Service – whether to family, community, or country – is the highest, noblest of callings.

The quality of service is vividly alive today in our sovereign, Queen Elizabeth II, who has reigned as Queen of Canada for more than sixty-three years, and in September 2015 succeeded Queen Victoria as the longest-serving monarch in British history. Much in our country has changed over those years, yet one aspect of Canadian life has remained true: Her Majesty the

Queen has spent the past six-plus decades showing Canadians the very meaning of constancy and service.

One can see that heightened sense of service in the duty and professionalism of the men and women in our armed forces. These professionals – and the veterans who preceded them – have answered the call to service. Their families serve too in their special way, with many of them having lost loved ones in service to our country.

The men and women who have earned the Order of Canada, our country's highest civilian honour, also serve. They express service through different disciplines of human endeavour – a wide spectrum of triumph that spans science, athletics, business, advocacy, public service, health care and medicine, journalism and broadcasting, culture, and the performing arts. While the fields and accomplishments of these Canadians differ, they are united in a singular desire to use their talent, wisdom, and generosity to enrich our country and enhance the lives of their fellow citizens. In doing so, these people mirror the motto of the Order – they desire a better a country.

Most of these men and women are not born to wealth or privilege. They have come from the ranks of millions of Canadians. I see examples of service from these people every day in cities and towns across the country. I am not alone. Anyone who has achieved any degree of success and been placed in a leadership position will point to dozens of teachers, mentors, and coaches who have made them better persons along the way. In my case, they number in the hundreds.

As someone who worked for years in several universities in our country, I have always had a special admiration for the educators of this country. Cherish our teachers, I say.

Throughout my time as governor general, I have encouraged Canadians to serve. I have emphasized three specific areas of service: supporting families and children, reinforcing learning and innovation, and spurring philanthropy and volunteering. I stress these spheres of human life and endeavour because they are the three pillars of a smarter, more caring country. And I have seen my role as governor general as a bridge that brings people of all backgrounds and ages together to create that kind of country, a nation that will inspire not just Canadians but the entire world.

In acting as that bridge, I have especially enjoyed getting to know the youngest generation of Canadians. You are an exceptional group. Born in this century, you are living through an extraordinary moment in time, a hinge point in history. A time of profound globalization, of disruptive technological changes, of major demographic shifts, of momentous concerns related to our natural environment and of changing attitudes toward – and expectations of – governments and public services. Daunting challenges abound and yet so do opportunities for you young people to find answers.

Born in this country or new to it in your earliest years, you are the benefactors of an extraordinary inheritance – a nation in which all young Canadians can grow their talents to the maximum and in which all young Canadians can succeed and contribute, and therefore a country in which all young Canadians should serve to ensure those who follow inherit a smarter and more caring country.

Service to country shaped Canada. Service to families and communities sustains our country. And this tradition of service must carry us forward to reach that smart and caring country of which we all dream.

As you young people travel along that path, I ask you to recall the words that General the Right Honourable Georges Vanier spoke to conclude his inaugural address as governor general. He said, "In our march forward in material happiness, let us not neglect the spiritual threads in the weaving of our lives. If Canada is to attain the greatness worthy of it, each of us must say, I ask only to serve."

I wish you only the best.
David

Some 400,000 babies are born in Canada every year. Many more thousands of boys and girls arrive on our shores each year to make our country theirs too.

The Greatest of These Is Fairness

A salute to a friend who wouldn't have it any other way.

To Purdy Crawford

Dear Purdy,

Seems that life is just a little quieter with you gone. You must have been tickled by the tribute. So many people you touched came forward, declared to Bea and the children their gratitude and admiration for you, wrote to newspapers and in blogs, and entertained each other with your quips and a few of your sage observations about the state of the nation, your trust in human nature, and your belief in the potential of young talent.

The word most heard in all these reflections was *fairness.* That's the quality you brought effortlessly to everything you did, and because of this I'm tempted to say that you were a paragon of Canadian virtue. Sorry if this makes you blush up there, but

I can easily name the values you held dear, knowing that each of these is a value that we Canadians hold dear as a society. I'll start with the equality of opportunity and excellence – your twin belief that everyone should have the chance to achieve greatness and that everyone has a duty to shoot for it. Much has been made of your humble beginning as a coal miner's son (even though, as you routinely pointed out, most Nova Scotian families have coal mining somewhere in their backgrounds). But it's uplifting to remember that you began your academic career as a scruffy kid in a two-room rural schoolhouse and rocketed upward with scholarships to Mount Allison, Dalhousie, and Harvard. You benefited from – and always acknowledged – a society intent on propelling those with talent and drive, no matter how humble or obscure their beginnings. You were treated fairly – nothing more – and you paid that back by mentoring, sponsoring, and cajoling those who later turned to you for advice in ways that enabled them to reach for their own distant goals. You just made sure everyone had a fair chance, as you had.

That's really it, isn't it? The best and fastest way to get the most from hard-working people is first to make sure they're included. Everything depends on our not being blinded by anyone's sense of (or worse, claim to) privilege. To nearly all Canadians, that may sound unquestionably obvious – but it wasn't always so. You saw that it wasn't, and you made it so wherever you appeared.

Purdy, your devotion to fairness will never be forgotten. I miss you.

David

Purdy Crawford (1931–2014), a companion of the Order of Canada, is known widely in Canada as a quintessential corporate philanthropist and a caring and sensitive leader. One of our country's leading lawyers and entrepreneurs, he is honoured in both the Nova Scotia and Canadian business halls of fame. He was Mr. Johnston's mentor in law, and he and his wife, Bea, are godparents to Sharon, the Johnstons' third daughter. Purdy and Bea had agreed that should anything happen to Mr. and Mrs. Johnston, their five daughters would simply be swept up into the Crawfords' family of eight. Mr. Johnston delivered a eulogy at Purdy's funeral in August 2014.

They Believe in Hope

Paying tribute to Canada's journalists.

To Roland Michener

Dear Roland,

You would be thrilled by the evolution of the Michener Award for excellence in public-service journalism that you created in 1970. With each passing year, the award inspires an increasing number of nominees; the award ceremony to honour finalists and the winner is one of the more special gatherings at Rideau Hall. In addressing the hundreds who attended the forty-fifth annual celebration, I posed a question to the assembled journalists: Why do you do what you do? I didn't ask about what they do – which is to say research, write, and air significant news stories in the public interest. Nor did I search for answers about how they did what they do – cultivating sources, asking tough questions, and relentlessly chasing the facts. I wanted to get at something much more elemental.

I suspect journalists might answer my question this way: to tell the truth; to shine a light on important, untold stories; to give a voice to the voiceless; to hold the powerful to account. But those answers don't tell the whole story. They fail to get to the heart of the matter. The real reason they do what they do is because they believe in hope.

Journalists are often accused of being hard-boiled and cynical. But in fact, the very best journalists are the least cynical people among us. I have a sense that you, the father of a journalist, agree with me. They believe in right and wrong. They believe that people, while quite capable of doing the very worst to each other, are also capable of the very best. They believe in our country and in our ability to create a fair and just society. That's why they do what they do – because they believe in hope.

That's why they endure the long hours, the calls not returned, the half-truths, and the frequent spin. It's a job, yes, but there are other jobs they could be doing. They do theirs for the common good. When we read or listen to or watch news stories, we aren't really doing so to learn about some state of affairs in our military, our labour market, our health care system, or our democracy. Ultimately, we're not reading, watching, or listening to what they report but rather why they report. We're following because we, too, believe in the common good and in the promise of Canada. We, too, are full of hope and want this country to live up to its potential. We, too, want to build a smarter, more caring Canada. And sometimes, that means having the courage to face hard facts and tell unpleasant stories. Also known as bad news!

The best journalists are like gardeners, helping us weed the garden, allowing space for new plants to grow. They certainly know how to dig! And despite everything that's changed in the news industry in recent years – and that's a lot – the basic principles of good journalism have not changed. And they won't. Journalistic ethics and integrity will never go out of style.

Thanks to you – a man of high ethics and unimpeachable integrity – Canadians have a way to salute these men and women, and to inspire them to continue sharing their special brand of hope with us.

Your colleague,
David

The Right Honourable Daniel Roland Michener (1900–1991) served as governor general of Canada from 1967 to 1974. A lawyer, diplomat, member of Parliament, and Speaker of the House of Commons prior to being appointed governor general, he created the Michener Award for Meritorious Public Service Journalism while serving as governor general. The award honours his daughter, Wendy, a prominent journalist who died in 1970, and through her memory, recognizes excellence in her profession. Each year, the Michener Awards Foundation selects six finalists from a wide variety of nominees. An overall winner is announced at the annual awards ceremony held at Rideau Hall. The Michener Awards Foundation also uses the occasion to present fellowships in investigative journalism and in journalism education.

Step Up and Step Out

A culture of major giving.

To Prem Watsa

Dear Prem,

Canadians need to be more pretentious.

Let me explain, my friend. The people at Rideau Hall recently concluded a nation-wide consultation with experts in philanthropy. Those round tables brought to light many surprising facts. One stood out to me: Canadians refrain from making large philanthropic gifts for fear of being thought of as pretentious. If wealthy Canadians give at all, they often give quietly. The Canadian trait of humility is usually an attractive and commendable one. Not in this instance though. I think we Canadians need to shed our timidity when it comes to making large philanthropic gifts.

What steps could we take to encourage more Canadians of great wealth to make large philanthropic gifts, and in so doing develop a culture of major giving in our country? Some would argue, I'm sure, that we need to change our tax code to nurture this kind of culture. I don't want to go there right away. I think we can take other actions beyond those that require the participation of our governments. We need to step up and step out.

Stepping out means we need to become more innovative about how we give. Why innovative? As you are well aware, we're living through an extraordinary moment in time, a hinge point in history. It's a time of profound globalization, of disruptive technological changes, of major demographic shifts, of momentous concerns related to our natural environment, and of changing attitudes toward – and expectations of – governments and public services. The argument I've heard from many – and that I agree with – is that too much of major giving today perpetuates the status quo; it doesn't do enough to replace the status quo with a better state of affairs. Canadian giving needs to become much more innovative to reflect the new realities. Just as we must innovate in science, engineering, medicine, and education, Canadians must innovate in how we make major philanthropic gifts. We must use them to reach marginalized people and unaddressed collective needs. We must give in ways that ensure every single Canadian can reach his or her full potential and enjoy a life of dignity and meaning. Above all, we must give using increasingly effective and more ambitious methods to overcome the daunting challenges we face right now in our time.

What does stepping out look like? Here's an example. Members of the G7 Social Impact Investment Taskforce held their first meeting at Toronto's MaRS Centre for Impact Investing. These men and women used the gathering to gain a better understanding of how to harness private capital for public good while generating financial returns for investors. This kind of investing recognizes that Canada, like its G7 partners, faces significant social, environmental, and financial challenges. The scope and gravity of these challenges call on us to be innovative, because governments sometimes lack the ability or the flexibility to respond adequately. It's not that there isn't enough money in the world to address these challenges; it's that the money is tied up in financial markets, held as interest-earning investments rather than being deployed where it's needed most. No one has recognized this fact more than you do. Yet when we invest in helping people, communities, and countries overcome challenges – all while generating returns for investors – that's innovative giving.

This social finance is a great example of smart giving, not least because of its focus on measuring impact. Measuring enables us to chart progress, improve performance and communicate value. It also makes it possible for us to avoid unnecessarily duplicating efforts and administrative costs. How would this principle work in practice? If you want to use a major gift to support a good cause, job number one is to find a charity with the same aim. If there isn't one, job number two is to ask whether you might help an existing charity innovate to fulfill that particular aim. And, if you still can't find a match, job number three is to fill that gap with an entirely new charity.

Using innovative giving that upends the status quo – stepping out – is only one way to encourage more Canadians of great wealth to make large philanthropic gifts and develop a culture of major giving in our country. Another is mentorship, or stepping up. I'm thinking most here about mentoring supplied by top philanthropists from Canadian business. Our country's business elite stands on a different hill. You enjoy a splendid view that others can only imagine. And in your gaze, you can see earlier and more clearly how forces are shaping up and what may be done to take advantage of them. So what then, beyond your own growth and security, is your responsibility? You men and women have unique power. You possess rare knowledge, skills, and wisdom gained from a lifetime at the highest levels of Canadian business. You've shown fierce ambition, drive, and intelligence to reach the top of your game and stay there. You've cultivated rich networks of professional and personal contacts throughout the country. It's those traits, values, and relationships that have made you such successful business people, executives, investors, and entrepreneurs. I would like you to put those traits, values, and relationships to work to revolutionize philanthropy in our country. Think of it: just as ingenuity is the life force of business, the sciences, education, and virtually all other disciplines in our age, ingenuity must be the life force of philanthropy in Canada. I know it can. I want our country's top philanthropist business people to use all the tools, tricks, and techniques that have made them such successful leaders in Canada – all their knowledge, skills, and experiences, all their ambition, drive, and intelligence, all their professional and personal contacts – and use them to nurture the next generation of Canadian philanthropists.

Specifically, I urge them to widen the circle of giving by mentoring five young, successful business people or professionals to be ingenious philanthropists. You know how to get things done. You've proven it all your lives. As a generation of proven business leaders and philanthropists, use your unique power. Work with five young, successful protegés to really shake up philanthropy in Canada. And make sure many of them are women. Make a point of nurturing successful young female business people and professionals into ingenious philanthropists. Canadian women have always been at the forefront of truly transformative social changes in our country. Help women tap into the natural inclination toward equality, fairness, and sharing that lies within them.

Some may very well say my call to you and to other successful business leaders to step up and step out is brash or pretentious. That's fine with me. I'm all for appearing a little pushy if it encourages more Canadians of great wealth to make large philanthropic gifts and helps us to develop a culture of major giving in our country.

Yours in friendship,
David

Prem Watsa is founder, chairman, and chief executive of Fairfax Financial Holdings, one of Canada's largest and most successful holding companies. Prem was born and raised in India. His father, orphaned at thirteen and raised by Jesuits, eventually became a college principal. Prem earned a scholarship to attend the Indian Institute of Technology at Madras. Soon after graduation, he emigrated to Canada with $500 in his pocket to seek and make his fortune. Devout and generous, he gives regularly and abundantly of his time, talent, and treasure to many worthy causes. A member of the Order of Canada, he serves as trustee and advisor to many non-profit institutions and was chancellor of the University of Waterloo from 2009 to 2015.

A Generation Later

The choice for Canada has never been clearer.

To Marcel Côté

Dear Marcel,

If Quebec goes. . . That was the contingency we contemplated together a generation ago. Looking back over the years from then to now, I must say working on our book was among the most satisfying intellectual exercises of my academic life and one of my most important acts as a citizen of Canada and Quebec. I think we served the people of our province and country well by discussing what was at stake in the 1995 referendum – what we considered were the real costs of separation. Our book was an impartial examination and analysis of available facts, unhindered by any political or governmental ties, obligations, or promises. Therein lay its value. It was based on a simple yet earnest belief: as citizens in a liberal democracy, we should engage in reasonable, public debate to guide collective decisions. No fear mongering. No fanciful promises. No guesswork. Just an open discussion founded on evidence, commanded by logic, and tempered by good sense. What a concept!

We concluded that, for Quebec, the choice for Canada was a much superior option than separation. We based our verdict largely on the indisputable and significant truth that a thousand and one hooks attach Quebec and Quebeckers to Canada, and no mere decoupling of Quebec from Canada – even if that were possible – would automatically lead to a world in which the problems we share would suddenly, magically be easier to regulate and solve. If anything, those problems would become more pronounced and more intractable for each side, as the process of unfastening those many hooks would raise unforeseen challenges, generate ill feelings, and consume valuable effort and time needlessly. Frankly, who really knew what would have followed a yes vote? Most of the main political players in the drama have since admitted they didn't know which steps they would take, how, and when. I think the main outcome of a slim yes vote would have been extreme uncertainty and all the confusion and false steps that would have flowed from this state of doubt.

Canadians then and certainly now can do much better with their shared inheritance than resorting to national divorce. What has transpired in our country and our world since we wrote our book has only reinforced the wisdom of the decision made by Quebeckers. The challenges we face now are just as big and in some cases bigger than ever before: growing economic uncertainty and unrest around the world; the ongoing search for energy alternatives in an era of increasing climate change; the resurgence of international and domestic terrorism. At the same time, we are living through an extraordinary moment in time, a hinge point in history. Ours is a world that is flattening as the historical, cultural, and geographic differences of nations and peoples are becoming increasingly irrelevant. We Canadians are more resilient in the face of the pressures of this emerging world together than apart; more adept at adjusting to its dislocations together than apart; better equipped and positioned to take advantage of its opportunities together than apart. Nothing I'm aware of has occurred since 1995 to cause me to change my view and those we presented in our book. Everything I've learned since then only reinforces my opinion.

As I travel throughout Quebec and meet hundreds of Quebeckers, I'm convinced they agree with me. Unlike perhaps past generations, young Quebeckers especially are much more open to the world. Why would we, they say, choose to erect more borders around ourselves when people around the world are finding ways to tear them down or at least rise above them? Why would we want to impose any sort of limits on our identities and ambitions when people around the world are broadening theirs? Why would we desire confrontation and conflict over compromise and consensus when we know from history – our own and that of others – that compromise and consensus is the truest path to peace and prosperity? Like them, I believe compromise is a better option than confrontation. Actions and decisions made out of confrontation can be exhilarating.

But that feeling tends to be fleeting, often leading those who have made rash choices to then ask themselves, "Okay, now what?" Some I'm sure see compromise as boring, as uninspiring, as lacking adventure. Yet it's a quality we have shown works best for us, if not best period. Our shared life on this land has been built largely on acts of compromise that build consensus.

Could the people of Quebec survive as citizens of a fully independent and sovereign Quebec? Of course they could. Yet the problems Quebeckers face won't be solved by separation alone or anything that flows from it. Quebeckers won't find answers to their challenges – ones they share with all Canadians and that all Canadians join with them to solve – through promises and magic wands. We'll find the answers the way we always have in this country – through hard work, a strong sense of justice, equality of opportunity, and a drive for excellence. As we stated in our book, these are the ingredients that make up good societies – more than power and politicians, more than the configurations of our governments, even more than our social safety net. For holding this view, some in Quebec called me an extreme federalist when I assumed the role of governor general. I'm not exactly sure what that tag means. My guess is it means I'm convinced that Canadian federalism, despite its faults, works better than pretty much any other system of government in the world at preserving political unity, increasing social harmony, and boosting economic prosperity. Even more accurately and appropriately, it works for this country because our form of federalism has evolved – and continues to evolve – to take into account the changing nature and needs of our people. To upend our country is not itself impossible. But such a change will not make reality disappear, will not solve our problems automatically and immediately. Yet this action would most likely be very costly for Quebec and for Canada. And when it comes to these costs, as always, the less fortunate, the weakest, the most vulnerable among us would end up footing most of the bill.

For Quebeckers, the choice for Canada is a much superior choice. It was in 1995; today, a generation later, the choice has never been clearer.

With deepest thanks and admiration,
David

Marcel Côté (1942–2014) co-authored with Mr. Johnston *If Quebec Goes . . .*, an examination and analysis of the effects of separation on Quebec and Canada during the time Mr. Johnston was principal of McGill. Mr. Côté enjoyed a distinguished professional life that saw him serve in many roles in the private and public sectors. An economist, he taught for a number of years at universities in Montreal and Sherbrooke, advised provincial and federal political leaders, ran his own business, and served on the boards of many national and multinational companies and local charities. A prolific writer, he wrote, in addition to his book with Mr. Johnston, books on innovation, business growth, and urban development.

Home of the People

What Rideau Hall means to me.

To Thomas McKay

Dear Mr. McKay,

I'm sitting at my desk in your former Ottawa home writing you a letter about this grand old building. Where do I begin? I guess I should start by telling you what I'm doing here. Rideau Hall has been the home and workplace of Canada's governors general since the birth of Canada in 1867. You would hardly recognize the building if you were to see it now. Like the country itself, Rideau Hall has grown much bigger as the years have passed. Alas, haven't we all? Your original villa has been the foundation of many additions to accommodate offices, studies, kitchens, dining rooms, meeting spaces, family areas, and more.

The main building now spreads across nearly 10,000 square metres and includes some 170 rooms. The rooms range in shape and character from the stately ballroom to the wood-panelled warmth of the office of the governor general to the vividly coloured, distinctively contoured Tent Room.

Yet Rideau Hall is much more than the workplace of governors general and their staffs. Vincent Massey, our country's first native-born governor general, often spoke of the building's ability to act as an instrument for Canada and Canadians. I agree. Rideau Hall is – and has been for generations – a place for and of people. It is a gathering place for Canadian families on warm summer mornings and cold winter afternoons – to walk and picnic, ski and skate. It is a welcoming place for distinguished visitors from around the world – kings and queens, presidents and prime ministers. And newlyweds. The Duke and Duchess of Cambridge launched their first royal tour together at Rideau Hall, spending a delightful summer afternoon getting to know Canadians, especially a group of exceptional young volunteers. It is a meeting place in which Canadians mark historic occasions and honour the best among us for bravery and for achievement in the arts, sciences, volunteerism, and architecture. How fitting. In all these ways, Rideau Hall is a physical manifestation of our shared experiences as Canadians. You even get a sense of Canada by walking through the rooms and hallways of Rideau Hall. Strolling through them – vast in size, varied in look – is like traversing our great land.

If the walls of these many rooms could talk, what stories might we hear them tell about Canadians over the past 150 years here? We might take in the cheers of onlookers as Lord Stanley's sons play hockey on the Rideau Hall rink. We might make out Princess Patricia asking her father's advice on lending her name to a fledgling regiment heading to France during the First World War. We might discover what Lord Byng and Mackenzie King discussed during their historic talks in 1926 surrounding the dissolution of Parliament. We might catch the flutter and rustle of papers as Lord Tweedsmuir works diligently on his next book. We might listen in as the menu for the very first Order of Canada dinner is being decided. And we might delight in the shouts and laughter of my twelve grandchildren – and scores of other children over the years – as they chase each other through the halls and across the grounds, playing hide and seek.

You built Rideau Hall as a testament to your ambition and that of the city you helped found. I think you would be pleased to know it has come to represent a different kind of place: the home of the people of Canada.

Thank you.
David

Thomas McKay (1792–1855) was a businessman who helped build the Rideau Canal and found the City of Ottawa. In 1838, he built Rideau Hall on the western edge of more than a thousand acres he bought east of the intersection of the Rideau River and

Ottawa River. He also constructed a sawmill and gristmill on the land to encourage Scottish immigrants to settle there. McKay's original acreage is now the site of the village of Rockcliffe Park. More than 225,000 people visited Rideau Hall in 2014–15.

Fool's Wisdom

Know who you are.

To Kalliana King

Dear Kalli,

I think I've always known that young people can teach older folks plenty. You taught me a valuable lesson: age is no barrier to giving. All of us – whether we're eight or eighty – can give, because each of us has something special deep within us that is worth sharing. Your special something is your love of a friend, and you used that friendship to take action. I have told your story of giving, and what I've learned from it, to boys and girls across Canada to encourage them to follow in your footsteps and find their own ways to give of themselves for the benefit of others.

I'd like to return the favour, if I may, and share with you my ethical approach to life. It is inspired by the following lines:

To thine own self be true,
And it must follow, as day the night,
Thou canst not then be false to any man.

These three lines come from Act 1, Scene 3 of *Hamlet*, William Shakespeare's most famous play. They are words of advice from Polonius to his son Laertes, as the young man leaves Denmark to go to study in Germany. To me, Polonius's fatherly counsel is a mirror test. His words compel you to stand in front of a make-believe mirror, look into your eyes, and ask yourself, Who am I? What do I stand for? If you can answer those questions clearly and honestly, you can gain a true understanding of who you are. That's not to say you'll know everything about yourself at one glance. You should ask these questions of yourself regularly over the course of growing up to clarify and reinforce your self-awareness. As you gain this knowledge, you will acquire a very practical way to make choices and decisions throughout life. You know exactly how you should act when you know precisely who you are.

I used Polonius's words often with my five children as they were growing up, telling them that most decisions, many of which can appear tricky at first glance, aren't really so difficult when you have a clear sense of who you are. All decisions don't become absolutely straightforward, but the mental and emotional distance you must travel from a situation to a decision becomes more direct and therefore faster to travel. Life presents us with lots of complications, but being true to thine own self enables you to settle a lot of questions the right way.

What's most surprising about these words is their source. While Polonius is an advisor to the King of Denmark, Hamlet refers to him as a "tedious old fool." As occurs many times in Shakespeare's plays, the fool is often the person who expresses the greatest wisdom. "To thine own self be true" are the wise words of Polonius. It is one fool's wisdom you can count on.

Your friend,
David

Kalliana King is the youngest recipient of the Governor General's Caring Canadian Award (now the Sovereign's Medal for Volunteers), which recognizes Canadians who have made significant, sustained, unpaid contributions to their communities in Canada or abroad. She was part of the group of twenty-eight recipients of the award when Mr. Johnston re-launched it in 2012. From a very young age, Kalliana – known as Kalli to her family and friends – has shown singular compassion for those living with muscular dystrophy, a compassion inspired by her friend who lives with the disorder. When she was eight years old, Kalli asked her parents for permission to become actively involved in fundraising. She dyed her hair pink to capture public attention, then shaved it off to raise funds for the cause. She has since gone door to door, participated in fundraising walks, and joined the local firefighters' charitable campaign. Through her efforts, she has raised $14,600, has inspired others in her region to give, and has raised public awareness of muscular dystrophy.

Take Care of the Rocks

Make room in life for the important things.

To winners of the Governor General's Academic Medal

Dear winners of the Governor General's Academic Medal,

Northrop Frye – a great teacher and scholar – wisely pointed out that graduation from an institution of higher learning is one of the four epic moments in a person's life – the other three being birth, marriage, and death. I think he's right. Birth, of course, is the start of all our journeys. Graduation and marriage represent milestones at which our lives gain momentum and move in wonderfully exciting and sometimes wholly unexpected directions. Trust me there. As for death, each of us has our own interpretation where that journey leads. Not even someone who was governor general can be dogmatic in answering that deep question. Yet as someone who has reached three of Professor Frye's milestones – and is in no great hurry to get to the fourth – I figure I'm in a pretty good position to pass along some friendly advice to you.

Now, even though I'm a teacher by trade, I'm not going to give you a lecture. You've probably heard enough of those recently to last you some time. The best teaching and learning tool ever devised is a good story. So here goes mine.

> A philosophy professor stood before her students with a number of items in front of her: a very large empty jar, some rocks, a box of pebbles, a box of sand, and a cold can of Coke. She picked up the empty jar and proceeded to fill it up with the rocks. She then asked her students if the jar was full. They agreed it was.
>
> The professor then picked up the box of pebbles and poured them into the jar. She shook the jar lightly. The pebbles, of course, rolled into the spaces between the rocks. She then asked the students again if the jar was full. The students weren't dummies. They smiled knowingly as they began to understand where the professor was going.
>
> The professor then picked up the box of sand and poured it into the jar. Of course, the sand filled up whatever small bits of room were left in the jar.
>
> Her demonstration, she explained, was like life. The rocks are the big, important things – your family, your partner, your children, your health,

and your education – anything that is so important to you that, if it were lost, you would be devastated. The pebbles are other things that matter but not as much as the rocks, such as a house or car or job. The sand is everything else, she said, the countless trivial little things in life.

If you put the sand or pebbles into the jar first, there is no room for the rocks. The same goes for your life, the professor continued. If you focus all your time and energy on the small stuff, you'll never have room in your lives for the things that are most important to you. So pay attention to the things that are critical to your happiness, the professor concluded. There will always be time for the little things. Take care of the rocks first, the things that really matter. Set your priorities. The rest is just sand.

Of course, one last item remained on the professor's desk. One student asked, "What about the can of Coke?" Now it was the professor's turn to smile. She opened it, poured it into the jar, and said, "Never forget to take the time to share a cool drink with a friend."

My story is straightforward and its lesson uncomplicated. Yet it's a story whose lesson is worth remembering and reflecting upon regularly. I imagine that some of you might have a cold drink or two with friends to celebrate your graduation from college or university – an epic event in your lives. Just a wild guess! While you're having that drink, start thinking about how you're going to take care of the rocks in your lives. You're chock full of knowledge, skills, and experiences that you have gained here at this institution of higher learning, filling each of your journeys ahead with amazing promise.

Like me, you're also privileged to live in a country that cherishes peace, freedom, democracy, justice, and equality and opportunity for all. These treasured Canadian values – so often taken for granted – will serve you well as you travel to your next big milestone in life. Yet what you have gained here at your school and those enduring Canadian values constitute a two-way street. There is a give as well as a take. So I pose this question to you and urge you to reflect upon it: How are you going to use your knowledge, skills, and experiences and the bedrock values on which they rest to create a smarter, more caring country?

You might be thinking: "Why is he asking me? I'm young. And why now? I'm just starting my career."

To those questions, I respond: Yes, you're young, but you have the mix of energy, ambition, and ideas that our country needs. And yes, you're just starting out, but your country needs you to begin using your talents today.

As recipients of the Governor General's Academic Medal, you have shown that combining hard work, perseverance, and commitment leads to academic success. I ask you now to use your time and talents in the service of others and of the broader community. I also urge you to think innovatively and creatively in all that you do, seeking new and better ways to solve problems and improve our lives. I challenge you to use your talents to build a better Canada. Just imagine the impact we would have if each recipient of this medal directed his or her intellectual talents in innovative ways. Together, you can help create a smarter, more caring Canada and a fairer, more just world. Think of it as one of the rocks you must place in your jars.

My sincerest congratulations to you all,
David

Governor General's Academic Medals have recognized the outstanding scholastic achievements of students in Canada for more than 140 years. Lord Dufferin, Canada's third governor general after Confederation, created the Academic Medals in 1873 to encourage academic excellence across the nation. Since then, they have been recognized as the most prestigious award that students in Canadian schools can receive. They are awarded to the student graduating with the highest average from a high school, as well as from approved college or university programs. Pierre Trudeau, Tommy Douglas, Kim Campbell, Robert Bourassa, Robert Stanfield, and Gabrielle Roy are just some of the more than fifty thousand people who have received the distinctive medal as the start of a life of accomplishment. Today, the Governor General's Academic Medals are awarded at four distinct levels: Bronze at the secondary school level; Collegiate Bronze at the post-secondary, diploma level; Silver at the undergraduate level; and Gold at the graduate level. Medals are presented on behalf of the governor general by participating educational institutions, along with personalized certificates signed by the governor general. The governor general writes an individual letter to each recipient capturing the core service messages articulated in this letter.

A New Band of Brothers and Sisters

The modern face of duty, courage, and honour.

To the women and men of the Canadian Armed Forces

To the extraordinary women and men
of the Canadian Armed Forces,

As members of one of the most respected institutions in the world, it must seem ironic to serve in the Canadian military and be aware that Canadians know so little about you.

Don't get me wrong. They know of your skill and dedication. They know of your devotion to duty and your commitment to the values of our country. They know of your bravery under near-impossible circumstances. They likely know people who have been rescued by you – at sea, in the woods, even out on the northern ice. They've certainly seen images of the life-saving work you've done in the field hospitals of far-flung nations. They've watched you take on terrorists, insurgents, invaders, and pirates. They have stood silent as you returned from long campaigns and bloody battles – sometimes on foot, sometimes in caskets – and they know deep in their hearts that your willingness to pay the ultimate price for our peace and freedom sets you in a category of your own.

Yet unless one has served Canada as a member of the military oneself, it is almost impossible to grasp either the depth of culture or strength of community that binds you together. As I write, the military in Canada is a family of 120,000 or so women and men from virtually every corner, every ethnic and linguistic group, every discipline, and every denomination of the country. And yet it functions with a unique internal coherence that few organizations enjoy – even the defence organizations of other nations. Why is that? I'd like to take a crack at answering that question by exploring four characteristics that set the Canadian military apart.

You are rooted in history. We don't often say it so overtly, but much of Canada's early history is military history. Our First Nations evolved military systems to conduct offensive and defensive operations in support of their societies at a level of sophistication that astounded early European explorers and settlers. Indeed, our vast geography, complex water systems, and deep forests required stealth tactics that French and English regiments were forced to learn from their native allies and put into swift practice lest they perish, instead of standing as they long had (arguably far too long) in tidy rows of targets in brightly coloured uniforms.

But the history of warfare and the history of the military are often usefully seen as distinct. In the settlement and growth of Canada from the 1600s on, it was the military that performed the critical function of surveyors, engineers, architects, surgeons, and builders of the towns and forts, ships and boats, canals and bridges that together were the vital links we used to forge a peaceful and prosperous new society.

Is it so different now? Even a casual glance at a list of the more than eighty current Canadian defence occupations reminds us that beyond the purely military disciplines, our uniformed citizens on land, sea, and air are experts in aerospace science, telecommunications, electrical engineering, geomatics, avionics, firefighting, health care, remote imaging, meteorology, pharmacology, search and rescue, international logistics, social work, and environmental science. The legacy continues.

Canada's growth as an independent nation owes much to our military history as well. An iconic example of this independence is the battle at Vimy Ridge in 1917. In 2012, I had the great honour and moving experience of addressing several thousand people – a huge number of visiting Canadian students, who paid their own way, among them – who had gathered at Vimy on the ninety-fifth anniversary of that horrible yet transformative struggle. The words I spoke on that anniversary tell the tale:

We stand on hallowed ground – a place of agonized conflict, a site of appalling loss of life, a vessel of sorrow, a crucible of courage, a hallmark of ingenuity, collaboration and resolve undertaken by men at arms in the cause of peace.

This is the final resting place of 3,600 men; a much-revered, far-flung patch of Canada some 4,000 kilometres from our closest shore. The battle that took place here on this long, deceptively low slope is for Canada and all Canadians an indelible memory. It is an unfading, undying symbol of who we are. It is a military engagement unlike any other in our history, for something deeply special happened here on this hallowed ground ninety-five years ago.

After their allies failed for months to take the ridge – at a cost of some 300,000 dead and wounded – the Canadians now in charge realized that numbers alone wouldn't be enough to carry the day. Radically different steps needed to be taken. So the men of the Canadian Corps went to work.

They built models and courses that simulated the battlefield and then studied those models and drilled on those courses relentlessly.

They devised and exhaustively rehearsed an intricately calibrated creeping barrage of artillery shells to insulate the infantrymen who would advance up the slope.

They combined expert use of the latest scientific methods and hard-won battlefield intelligence to locate, target, and eventually destroy the enemy's heavy guns and mortar emplacements.

And most importantly, the Canadian entrusted with operational authority of the fight – General Arthur Currie – did something ingenious and highly risky. He entrusted every soldier under his command – all four divisions of the Canadian Corps – with the whole battle plan. Nothing was hidden from the men. No risk. No peril. No agenda. No expectation. In the weeks leading up to the battle's start on the morning of April 9, 1917, every Canadian soldier – from colonel to private – was given the big picture and asked to help make every detail of the plan and the action better.

Currie's trust did more than acknowledge and motivate the troops as colleagues in a greater cause. That trust in the rank and file of the Canadian Corps showed a caring for and respect of fighting men that was rarely if ever seen at that time. That trust also tapped deeply into the authentic Canadian experience of equality, collegiality, community, and interdependence – qualities that living in our vast and somewhat unforgiving country demanded of us for mere survival. And by calling on that profound wellspring of ingenuity and compassionate collaboration – a strategy very much taught to immigrant European settlers by our country's Aboriginal peoples – Currie inspired his incredibly tenacious men to bring forth the best that Canadians have to give.

What should all Canadians recognize and remember ninety-five years later – ninety-five years after the single bloodiest day in Canadian military history? We recognize and should always remember that out of the staggering death and destruction of that battle, out of the stunning carnage of that day, out of the cruellest conflict in our national life, we Canadians have been able to grasp and carry forward something that is true and honourable and lasting: that we are a smart and caring nation, that to prosper we must become ever smarter, ever more caring, and that when we work together in a spirit of ingenuity and compassion, the best that Canadians have to give the world is the best that anyone can give.

You are a flexible, rapidly evolving institution. Among other things, the lesson we learned at Vimy is that it is better to invite the involvement and input of everyone on a mission than rely on the leadership alone. As governor general and your commander in chief these past years, I have travelled across Canada and around the world to visit you and your comrades in action in almost every possible kind of operation, and I have been struck again and again by the depth of education and degree of cross-training you can rightly boast, and the respect in which you are held by your superior officers and your peers around the world. Perhaps it is a bit like Canadian actors in Hollywood, who are not stereotyped as their American equivalents are, precisely because to succeed in the smaller Canadian film and television industry they had to master every type of role. So too our military (at perhaps one-twentieth the size of the U.S. military) has had to favour broad training over rigorous specialization, creating a flexible force of professionals who can do just about anything and do it well.

One could say that from the moment we took over direct military command of our own forces from the British Crown in Council in 1906, we've been changing. Our flexibility has led to an extraordinary range in the kinds of operations we've been able to undertake. Since the Second World War, we have punched well above our weight in more than two hundred missions worldwide, with some seventy of those being international partnerships. You – our soldiers, sailors, and aviators – are considered world-class professionals and have been identified by foreign heads of state and military leaders alike for your unique and conspicuous service wherever you are deployed.

You are a disciplined yet compassionate society. Wherever you have served, you have served with courage, sacrificed your lives, and endured the extremes both of climate and of separation from family and friends. Through it all, you have proved your diligence, your toughness, and your compassion for the plight of others. Your latest and most furious campaign was a telling example of these qualities. How well I remember the day you returned after more than a dozen years of our Canadian mission in Afghanistan – a mission with a certain aim, yet in an operational theatre that threw everything it had at you.

Afghanistan tested your head, your heart, and your gut. As soldiers, you dug deep, putting all your training into practice, and learning new tactical skills on the move – skills that will form the training of the generation of soldiers who are readying themselves now to meet the high standards that you have set. You saw the suffering of a population under the tyranny of deliberate violence, enforced poverty, and perverse fanaticism. Many of you witnessed the worst and the best of humanity, and while you all brought home images that will haunt you, you carry also the memories of encounters that will inspire you for the rest of your lives. Through it all, you put yourselves at ultimate risk, standing your ground in defence of your beliefs, getting the job done so that those you came to help got that help. Even as your colleagues were injured or lost in the line of duty, you soldiered on. For that, as always, all Canadians stand in deepest respect.

Over the course of this mission, you undertook many roles: as soldiers foremost, but also as ambassadors, peacekeepers, protectors, and rebuilders of civil society, and as teachers to Afghan's own security force. Many talents, many roles: that versatility is a Canadian legacy and, I believe, one of the greatest assets we had on the ground.

You are a magnet for people who believe in duty, courage, and honour. Whenever I meet young people who have recently joined the Forces, I am struck by their strength of character.

They are all volunteers. They are ready to contribute. They radiate enthusiasm. They are alert and interested. They are respectful without being timid. Without doubt, the education and training programs of our military are powerful incentives for potential recruits, but I've seen and spoken with too many not to know that their real goal is to join one of the best teams out there. Their earliest role models have often been relatives who have served – perhaps a sibling, uncle, aunt, or parent. As young people watch these mentors radiate their intelligence, confidence, spirit of adventure, and sense of belonging, the seeds of interest are sown.

In our Forces, what you must give is what you get back, and I contend that this combination of contribution and reward can be summed up in three important old words: duty, courage, and honour. Duty is your moral obligation to do what is required of you. Courage is your drive to carry on when that requirement puts you at risk. And honour is your deep sense of doing these things to the highest and most ethical standards of conduct. In the new band of brothers and sisters we call the Canadian Armed Forces, duty, courage, and honour are both the hallmark of your behaviour and the greatest appeal to those who will fall in to march with you in the future.

Dear comrades in arms, I salute you, commend you, and thank you for being the epitome of our country's best qualities.

David Johnston

The men and women of Canada's military have served as Canada's builders, protectors, and ambassadors since the seventeenth century.

The Good Society

Build trust in governance.

To Stephen Jarislowsky

Dear Stephen,

Thank you and Gail for receiving me so graciously in your home and sharing your ideas. I saw our discussion as a continuation of our intriguing conversations while salmon fishing on the British Columbia coast. I'm sending you this note to ascertain whether I've grasped the three basic elements of our idea of the good society in Canada: ethics, trust, and excellence in public and corporate governance.

Personal and professional ethics, and the trust that ethical behaviour breeds in our fellow citizens, is a subject and cause that animates you. You indicated that all of the world's great religions are based essentially on the golden rule: do unto thy neighbour as you would have your neighbour do unto you. You've lived your life according to this fundamental rule and in the spirit that human nature is inherently good. We agree, however, that authority not founded on ethics is dangerous for people and societies. In the wrong hands, particular religions and belief systems can do a lot of damage to subvert the golden rule by casting the "neighbour" as an enemy and then arguing that a strong nationalistic state or tribe is required to repel and conquer that dangerous, alien neighbour. As I write these lines, I'm reminded of a trenchant observation made by C.S. Lewis many years ago: "I am very doubtful whether history shows us one example of a man who having stepped outside traditional morality and attained power has used that power benevolently."

Ethics as a precursor to trust is evident in your life's actions and decisions. You mentioned that the so-called secret to your advice being sought and accepted by people and groups so often through your nearly nine decades of life is that you have no concern for personal gain in the matter under consideration. People trust you and your ideas, because you have no self-interest from the outset other than acting ethically. Your moral principles forge and harden trust among those with whom you deal. You also realize that trust is a fragile quality. Trust, therefore, is built through a lifetime of actions and decisions inspired by the highest ethical principles: fairness, openness, honour, duty. By way of contrast, you remarked that, at your recent reunion of the Harvard Business School, the dean reported that the school is now giving courses on ethics. In your formative years, ethics was not taught at school but was practised regularly by those of your generation – men and women who had lived through the Depression and the Second World War. Both of us are all for teaching, yet rules alone don't lead to ethical behaviour. Recent experience in the United States shows a pervasive willingness among some leaders in business, high finance, and law to ignore or look for ways around hard and fast rules. Ethics must be lived experiences first and foremost. Our moral principles are passed down from the old to the young through living. It is then up to the young to live these principles themselves. Ethics become more secure when they are truths embedded within us rather than directives codified in some manual.

To illustrate with an example, you referred to a remark made recently by a friend who is a lawyer and public servant in Quebec. She said there is a historical element in French Canadian thinking that making money and amassing wealth was inherently wrong and evil. Through your writings, speeches, and interviews, you have done much to change that thinking among young French Canadians. Your actions speak even louder than your words, though your words are vital to inspire and illustrate the actions. You've earned the trust of French-speaking Canadians by respecting their customs and culture, by supporting their art (the first paintings you showed me in your home were a fabulous collection by Jean Paul Lemieux), by involving yourself directly in their businesses and institutions, and by speaking their language well. That last point is not unsubstantial. As a person who speaks three languages fluently, you appreciate that learning and speaking the languages of others is a mark of respect and a powerful way to build trust.

Your professional life shows how the concepts of ethics and trust are intertwined. In our public life in Canada, we express these twinned ideals in how we govern our institutions. As an example, we spoke about the Canadian Coalition on Corporate Governance and the Institute on Fair Investing. These organizations manage about two and a half trillion dollars from pensions, investment funds, and other managed assets. Ohio University has recognized them both for excellence in good governance. Their principles are so respected that they have made their way into legal frameworks on corporate governance in Canada through influential reforms of various securities commissions and other capital market regulators across the country. Are they sustainable? Who knows? you said. What will endure is not entirely predictable, but the fact that they are institutionalized and part of the corporate cultures of the most important wealth-managing trustees in the country is a good start toward durability. Societies have been shaken disastrously when public trust in institutions is undermined or vanishes entirely. Greece is a recent example of what happens when the people of a country lose faith in public institutions as a consequence of the absence or perceived absence of ethics in the actions and decisions of political and financial leaders.

Excellence in governance extends beyond the political and financial, of course. Proof lies in your efforts to bring a modern and ethical governance model to Quebec hospitals. This model centres the activities of hospitals on patients, not doctors. It calls for executives being responsible for management of hospitals and strong boards to ensure the presence of active hands-on management and oversee efficient patient-centred activities. More particularly, you mentioned the Navigator program you helped establish at the Montreal General Hospital. By engaging several retired doctors and nurses, who know the hospital intimately, to manage, or navigate, various gates or blockages and move patients efficiently through to rapid successful treatment, the program enabled the hospital to reduce treatment time for lung cancer patients from 82 to 22 days. You indicated the model has been extended to patients suffering from several other cancer conditions, and you anticipate it can be replicated in other hospitals and health care institutions.

What can we do as a country to embed ethical behaviour in our people and institutions and thereby ensure that our leaders and the institutions they direct are trusted by Canadians? We talked a lot about the Order of Canada as one possible avenue. You remarked that there is extraordinary potential for good in the 3,200 or so recipients of the Order of Canada – for two reasons. First, recipients share a clear goal. That wish is captured in the Order's motto: they desire a better country. Second, unlike many of the world's honour systems, ours is non-political and based on merit. In this way, it does not perpetuate a class system; instead, it promotes equality of opportunity and excellence as mutually reinforcing qualities. You suggested that Order of Canada recipients should be encouraged to exchange ideas among themselves on what they continue to do to build a better country. These ideas could be grouped into mentorship initiatives, a speakers series in which recipients can share insights from their lives, and broad endeavours divided by disciplinary categories (the arts, science, volunteerism) that would stress ongoing local initiatives rather than one-off top-down projects. You also recommended no half measures – do the thing right or don't do it – and bringing in younger people, perhaps via a junior Order of Canada that does not turn on lifetime achievements but on some other more punctual criteria. At a minimum, you recommended we collect ideas from Order of Canada recipients – that from this much talent there have to be some extraordinary ideas.

We agreed that the reason for taking all these actions is that the Order of Canada is an excellent vehicle to promote ethics, engender trust, and build and maintain public institutions in which citizens have confidence. I think this is our purpose in the end, isn't it? Ethics, trust, and excellence in public and corporate governance create the good society we all want and deserve. If the effect of a life well lived is the drawing together of one's fundamental principles in the pursuit of something larger than oneself, then the Jarislowsky Effect, you might say, is that special combination of ethics in action and trust in our institutions that leads to the good society about which we spoke so much. Isn't that so? This is what I have learned from you, Steve. I believe it is what Canadians hope for in so many ways and what we fear we may be losing: that we do the right things and that we earn the trust of one another. This effect ought to be shared and advanced, not just between old friends like you and me, but also as a legacy for many to participate in. We should think about how to do just that and discuss the possibilities when we meet again. I would like that.

Thanks for what you do every day for Canada, my friend.
David

Stephen Jarislowsky is founder, chairman, and former chief executive officer of Jarislowsky Fraser Limited, one of the largest and most successful investment management firms in Canada. In 2002, he co-founded the Canadian Coalition for Good Governance to further the cause of business ethics. A companion of the Order of Canada and grand officer of the National Order of Quebec, he has received honorary doctorates from many Canadian universities and, along with his wife, has endowed many university chairs in Canada in disciplines as varied as history and biotechnology.

At the Heart

Summer at La Citadelle.

To Régis Labeaume

Dear Régis,

I'm writing you from one of my favourite places in all the land – La Citadelle in Quebec City. From this majestic structure, I look about and see a great deal literally and figuratively.

I gaze west across the waters of the St. Lawrence River – narrower here than at most spots along its course but still broad and deep – and I think of Samuel de Champlain and his leadership in founding the first permanent settlement in what would become Canada. The Aboriginal peoples of this region are also vivid in my mind, especially the Algonquin, whose word for the narrowing of the waters – Kebec – gave this city and province its name. A fitting choice of name for a wisely chosen site: Quebec City's position at the neck of the St. Lawrence would enable it to control for generations the traffic of people and goods from the Atlantic Ocean to deep within the Canadian interior and vice versa. Far below my gaze to the south sits the old city with its ancient port, basin, and winding lanes. Artemus Ward, an American humorist, wrote that these streets don't lead anywhere in particular yet everywhere in general. Within the maze of asphalt and cobblestones is Parc Montmorency, site of the Old Parliament Building wherein the Quebec Conference was held and leaders of the British North American colonies set down the building blocks of Canada's constitution – a historic gathering whose 150th anniversary I had the honour of celebrating with you and the people of the city by unveiling a statue of Étienne-Paschal Taché, the too-often-forgotten Father of Confederation, who was chairman of the conference. Extending east and north from my vantage point is the modern Quebec City, a mix of old and new: soaring towers, venerable churches, and the elegant symmetry of the Parliament Building, which today houses the province's national assembly. And turning again to the west spreads the grassy green Plains of Abraham, where two empires met one morning to determine the fate of half a continent.

Looking at Quebec City from this special perch atop Cap Diamant, therefore, I see not only the city you lead, but also the country we all love – its origins, its traditions, its growth, and its splendour. This city is the heart of Canada. In his book *Three Weeks in Quebec* – a history of the 1864 conference – Christopher Moore quotes American writer Henry

James recounting his train trip to this vital place. James describes "a dreary night journey through crude, monotonous woods" until the rail line reached the south shore of the St. Lawrence River and then "beyond it, over against you, on its rocky promontory, sits the ancient town, belted with its hoary wall and crowned with its granite citadel." James's use of that word – crowned – is perfectly fitting. La Citadelle surmounts the city physically, and from its founding in 1608 by Champlain until Confederation in 1867, Quebec City was the wellspring of the Crown in Canada, the sovereign authority in this land – first as the centre of New France and then as the seat of government for the Province of Canada and residence of the governor general of British North America. Lord Dufferin understood the importance of the Crown to Canada and therefore the significance of Quebec City and La Citadelle to our country. That understanding inspired our third governor general to make this old fortress the second vice-regal residence and to lead the effort to preserve much of the city's fortifications and defences. So if Quebec City is the heart of Canada, I believe La Citadelle is the heart of the city.

I am the current heir of this grand legacy. As you know, Sharon and I stay at La Citadelle for some weeks each year. This time is close to my heart. I cherish the ability being here gives me to experience the city and meet the people of Quebec City, as well as the many people from across Canada and throughout the world who choose it as a vacation destination. Wise people. La Citadelle remains a working site as well. Here our country's governors general grant awards, present honours for bravery and exceptional service, receive letters of credence from ambassadors and high commissioners, and inspect the honour guard of the Royal 22nd Regiment of the Canadian Armed Forces, whose home is La Citadelle and who recently celebrated their 100th anniversary. The history of the Van Doos mirrors much of that of our country – another reason that makes their home city so special and so representative of the whole nation.

This is what I see at the heart of the city at the heart of the country. Thank you for giving me this opportunity to share my view with you.

Heartily yours,
David

Régis Labeaume is mayor of Quebec City.

Birth of a Smart and Caring Nation

Making sense of Canada's sacrifice in the First World War.

To Larry Murray

Dear Larry,

War is the epitome of human failure. What is more damning an indictment against us than taking up arms against one another? The First World War is the ultimate example of the waste, futility, and shame of war: an estimated 37 million military and civilian casualties; an unprecedented destruction of homes and land; and an unconscionable squandering of economic resources and human potential. This cataclysm was the outcome of a clash of rival alliances of European powers that drew in Canada as a result of our country's close political, cultural, and social attachments to one of those powers. Our leaders showed nothing especially noble in making the decision to go to war. Loyalty perhaps? During the war and in the century since, Canadians have tried to extract some meaning from our participation in this conflict. That's understandable. Our country paid a stiff price in those four years. Some 620,000 Canadians were mobilized. They all sacrificed in some way: 67,000 gave their lives; 250,000 were wounded; untold numbers came home scarred not in body but in mind – some never to recover. What would these 67,000 have achieved had they not died in war? How would our country and this world be different? What value, beauty, and uniqueness were lost with their deaths?

We have no answers to these questions. Yet Canadians tried – and continue to try – to make some sense of such a terrific sacrifice. Gwynne Dyer, in his book *Canada in the Great Power Game*, outlines one meaning that has taken hold: "The war was portrayed in France and the English-speaking countries as a battle in defence of democracy, with the implication that a dark night of tyranny would descend on the world if the other side won. A hundred years after, the same rhetoric is still trotted out every Remembrance Day." Another popular attitude is that the war enabled Canada to come of age as a full-fledged country – that a distinctive Canadian nation separate from Great Britain emerged from the muck and mayhem of France and Flanders. Brigadier-General Alexander Ross, who commanded the 28th Battalion at Vimy Ridge, expressed that sentiment on behalf of his comrades and compatriots. Speaking about the Battle of Vimy Ridge, Ross said: "It was Canada from the Atlantic to the Pacific on parade. I thought then, and I think today, that in those few minutes I witnessed the birth of a nation."

As a navy man for many years and leader of this country's largest organization of veterans, you have had many occasions no doubt to share your insights on Canadians at war. I too speak about war and our country many times at home and abroad as governor general and commander in chief of the country's armed forces. The most poignant of these were the gatherings each Remembrance Day at Rideau Hall to honour the National Memorial (Silver) Cross Mother and, through her, the service and sacrifice of her child and all other sons and daughters who died serving their country. At all the memorial events I have attended, I tried to express revulsion for war and respect for the dedication, skill, and courage of the men and women we sent and send to it. On these occasions – especially in trying to find and express meaning for the First World War and our country's contribution to it – I did my best not to fall back on comforting but false beliefs. We are not a nation of mythmakers. I like what historian Tony Judt wrote in that regard: "A well-organized society is one in which we know the truth about ourselves collectively, not one in which we tell pleasant lies about ourselves." Canada is, in Judt's words, a well-organized society, and the best way we honour the men who fought in the First World War – and the men and women who still fight – is to tell the truth as best we can. Was the First World War our true birth as a nation? I think that's a little too neat and tidy an explanation. I lean toward the opinion offered by historian

Jean Martin: "If Canada was born in the trenches of France and Belgium between 1915 and 1918, it was only in the minds of a few thousand soldiers who had very shallow roots in our country. In the minds of most of its inhabitants, Canada had already existed for a long time."

While the First World War did not give rise to a new nation, what it did, I think, was create in Canadians, especially those who served, a confidence in their own thinking and methods. These Canadians saw the destruction and horror that British and European ways brought about. On the flip side, they saw the success that our thinking and methods could bring. In a 1920 article, W.S. Wallace wrote: "In the Great War, the maple leaf badge came to be recognized as the symbol of a strong national spirit which never failed before any task with which it was confronted, and which contributed in a substantial measure to the breaking down of the German defences in the latter half of 1918." We lost faith in their methods and gained it in ours. This thinking then began to influence Canadian life at home. My wife's grandmother was the matron of the hospital in Lethbridge, Alberta, right after the war. She told me that she and her colleagues in her hospital began thinking much more critically about methods and approaches to care and administration as a result of Canada's wartime experience. To put a finer point on it, I think the war was proof to all Canadians of our desire and capability to be what I call a smart and caring nation.

We believe that to prosper we must become ever smarter, ever more caring, and that when we work together in a spirit of ingenuity and compassion, the best that Canadians have to give the world is the best that anyone can give.

Lest we forget.
David

Larry Murray is grand president of the Royal Canadian Legion, the largest veterans service organization in Canada. A member of the Royal Canadian Navy for thirty-three years, he captained several vessels, headed up Maritime Command, and served as acting chief of the Defence Staff. Mr. Murray retired in 1997 with the rank of vice admiral, spending the next ten years occupying executive roles in Canada's public service. He earned many honours, awards, and decorations during his distinguished military and civilian careers. Foremost among them is being named a member of the Order of Canada.

What Will Your Gift Be?

Celebrating Canada at 150.

To the citizens of Canada

Dear Citizens of Canada,

When I visited the *imagiNation 150* office in Calgary during one of my first trips as governor general, I was captivated by that organization's raison d'être: Canada's special birthday in 2017 calls for Canadians to give their own special gifts to our country – gifts that kindle our collective spirit and make our country even better. Since that day, I've taken every opportunity possible to ask Canadians, "What will your gift be?" It's my way to encourage Canadians to start thinking about the gifts they will give their country when we celebrate the 150th anniversary of Confederation, and to make sure they follow through on their thinking when 2017 rolls around.

Canadians shouldn't be content only with erecting cultural monuments or other publicly funded infrastructure to mark this occasion. Nor is there any reason why Canadians should wait for their governments to encourage and mobilize them to give. Pierre Berton, in his book *1967: The Last Good Year*, outlined the many ways Canadians marked the centennial of our country. What struck me most was the message CBC personality John Fisher gave during his cross-country tour of Canada leading up to the event. "The Centennial belongs to you!" he said. "Do something. It doesn't matter how small your effort is!"

An occasion as momentous as Canada 150 comes along once – maybe twice – in a lifetime. This anniversary is a rare opportunity for Canadians to do something special for their country, to give a gift to Canada. As governor general, I've crisscrossed the country, meeting and speaking with Canadians of all ages, and backgrounds, and I've asked them to think deeply about what their gifts might be. Now is the time to put plans in motion. Now is the time to turn ideas into action. Now is the time to act. The country we dream of won't build itself.

Each Canadian has the power within him or her to give something special to our country and help build that country we dream of. Big or small, complex or simple – it doesn't matter what Canadians give. The gift each Canadian chooses is as unique as the person who shares that gift. I especially like the range of opportunities the 150th anniversary offers to young Canadians to express their imaginations and creativity. I would go so far as to say that young people in our country have a special responsibility to lead our country's celebration of the

150th anniversary of Confederation – for two reasons. First, our country will be theirs to shape in the 50 years from 2017 until 2067 – our country's bicentennial. Second, birthdays belong naturally to the young. In our country's Centennial year, 55 per cent of Canadians were under the age of 30, so young people then were in a perfect position, by virtue of their sheer numbers, to influence the celebrations. That percentage is now 36. Our country is nearly 50 years older, and so are Canada's people as a group – and getting older on average with each passing year. Young people in Canada today are going to have to work much harder and think much deeper if they are to guide our coming party.

I know they are up to the task. In fact, I have on many occasions challenged these young people and all Canadians to come up with three truly special gifts for Canada. I've challenged them to take their knowledge, skills, and experiences, their ambition, drive, and intelligence, their personal and professional connections and use them to carry out three giving moments to celebrate this special anniversary of their country.

I know that, in approaching 2017, all Canadians will draw inspiration from the challenge laid before them by Lord Byng many years ago. Our country's twelfth governor general called on Canadians "to be as big, with minds as large and souls as great as the land in which we live." I echo my predecessor's evocative words and the ambitious spirit behind them.

What will your gift be?
David

At the time of writing, there were 35,870,000 Canadians living in the country. If each of them brings a present to the celebrations in 2017, it will be quite a party.

The Idea of Canada

A nation for all nations.

To John Buchan, Lord Tweedsmuir

Your Excellency,

I address you formally out of respect. Yet I feel like I know you as a friend despite the years that separate our lives and tenures in office, and despite the fact you died a year before I was born. While I draw inspiration and ideas from many of my predecessors, the experiences and lessons from your life and specifically from your term as governor general are my guiding light. In your quiet way, you established a new model for the position of governor general in our country. Unlike your predecessors, you travelled widely across this country, especially to the North, to meet Canadians in the places where they lived, worked, worshipped, and played. The humanity and compassion you showed encouraged them to exhibit these qualities in their own lives. And while you were an unusually engaged citizen of the world, your country was a country of the mind, as Frank Scott put it.

You also made the first substantial contribution to the country's cultural life by setting up the Governor General's Literary Awards. How appropriate for someone who had over a hundred and twenty books published in his lifetime. Your awards have grown into Canada's most coveted prize for writers, translators, and illustrators, and the ceremony to honour winners is a highly anticipated gathering at Rideau Hall each year. Your example inspired other ways to honour and inspire Canadians, such as creating the Governor General's Performing Arts Awards, the Governor General's Innovation Awards and the Polar Medal, as well as rekindling the Governor General's Caring Canadian Award, which in 2015 was elevated to the Sovereign's Medal for Volunteers.

What impresses me most about you and your tenure is the sensitivity you showed to the country's French and British heritage and the wise words you shared with all Canadians in the crucial first decade following passage of the 1931 Statute of Westminster. This act of the British Parliament, which granted legislative independence to Canada and made it a fully sovereign country under the law, stirred in many Canadians a sense of unease about their identity and more precisely an uncertainty about where their primary loyalty should lie – with Britain or with Canada or somewhere in between.

While you recognized the limitations placed on your office and how these limits often compelled you to speak in "governor generalities," you nonetheless spoke clearly and sharply enough to persuade Canadians that having multiple loyalties was a positive force, and that we should acquire ever-widening loyalties, especially as we grew older. We should start small, you said, with our schools and neighbourhoods, and broaden our loyalties to include the profession in which we work and serve, then the province and nation in which we live, and ultimately our whole world and fellow human beings. You said that this array of loyalties was a positive and essential force not only in this country, but also throughout a world that had recently been drawn into a cataclysmic war by violent, exclusionary nationalisms, and that would soon be engulfed in an even more catastrophic war by these same forces. Why must we pay such an awful price to learn our lessons?

You had a keen view of this country. Perhaps it came from the fact that you were new to it and therefore could see it with fresh eyes. Early in your tenure, you observed that Canadians had a limited vision – that "everybody thinks in compartments" of region or language or religion or ancestry. You taught us that we don't need to shed any other aspect of our identities to be Canadian. Being Canadian isn't a matter of choosing a single compartment. Canadians become their true selves when they remain open to the world and all the complexity it represents. When we do so, we lessen if not overcome the many surface divisions and centrifugal forces that would tear apart such a diverse country as ours. Inclusiveness and an acceptance of complexity and all the difficulties and ultimately richness it brings: that is your idea of Canada. At the same time, you were under no illusions about the challenge Canadians faced to embody this idea of the nation. Canada is, after all, "a biggish job."

Hugh MacLennan opens his novel *Two Solitudes* – published in 1945 but with its narrative spanning 1917 to 1939 – by exploring the habit of Canadians back then to think in compartments:

> Two old races and religions meet here and live their separate legends, side by side. If this sprawling half-continent has a heart, here it is. Its pulse throbs out along the rivers and railroads; slow, reluctant and rarely simple, a double beat, a self-moved reciprocation.

He was writing about Montreal specifically, yet his words speak to the entire country and the compartments in which we placed ourselves then and in which some of us still choose to dwell or encase others – French-speaking or English-speaking, Protestant or Catholic or Muslim, new Canadian or native born, urban or rural, young or old, male or female. Many read the novel then and even now as a verdict on Canada: a country forever divided and therefore doomed. I disagree. Any of our differences are not symptoms of a permanent condition. We Canadians have shown an uncanny ability to bridge distinctions and include the isolated. John Ralston Saul wrote that

Two Solitudes offered that differences weren't prisons, merely complications that could be dealt with. MacLennan's idea of Canada is that our history is itself an exercise in dealing with complications that come with life in such a vast, diverse country. The differences are there and may always exist in some form. Let's deal with them and overcome them. Better yet, rise above them.

Both you and MacLennan held the idea that Canada has always been an experiment increasingly devoted to the proposition that ours would be home to all the peoples of the world – a nation for all nations. How has your idea fared over the past seventy-five years? I tried to answer this question in the preamble to the Speech from the Throne to open the Second Session of the Forty-first Parliament. My idea of Canada is that we have been able to survive and thrive because we have embraced some qualities larger and more important than others that may seem different on the surface.

We are inclusive. We are 36 million people gathered from every part of the world. We welcome the contribution of all those who inhabit this land – from the first of us to the latest among us.

We are honourable. People of peace, we use our military power sparingly, but when we do so we do so with full conviction, gathering our forces as men and women who believe that the freedoms we enjoy cannot be taken from us. This clarity focuses our might in terrible times. And wherever and whenever we unleash that might, we raise our grateful voices and our prayers to honour those who have stood in harm's way for us.

We are selfless. Our survival has been sustained by humility and acceptance of our mutual interdependence. Giving lies in our very nature, certain in our hearts that none but the gift passed from an open hand will multiply as those we help better themselves, those they love, and, at length, the country they call home.

We are smart. We deplore self-satisfaction, yearning rather for self-improvement. We love learning and cherish our right to it. We are united, prosperous, and free precisely because we ensure that Canadians have opportunities to learn, excel, advance, and thus to contribute.

We are caring. Our abiding concern for the common good of our neighbours in each community makes us responsive. We do not abandon our fellows to scrape by in times of distress or natural disaster. Inspired by our common bond, we come swiftly and resiliently to the aid of those in need.

I think you would agree with this fresh idea of Canada. Even more so, I think you would agree that Canadians must relentlessly uphold principles and take actions that are inclusive, honourable, selfless, smart, and caring at every turn without fail. So much for governor generalities!

Collegially yours,
David

John Buchan, His Excellency the Right Honourable the Lord Tweedsmuir (1875–1940), served as Canada's fifteenth governor general from November 2, 1935, to February 11, 1940, the day of his death.

Acknowledgements

These letters reflect my thoughts, as they have developed over the years, about the many varied qualities that make our nation unique. That thinking has been informed by an ever-widening circle which has enriched and sustained me: family, friends, colleagues, teachers and students. They, in their own various ways, are co-authors of this book and I am enormously grateful for their continuing inspiration.

In writing these letters, I had the support of a small, remarkable team: Brian Hanington and John Phillips whose insight and long experience inform each of the letters; Mike Caesar, Yonatan Lew and Annabelle Cloutier who assist me with many of my speeches; Lois Claxton and Stephen Wallace who guided the execution of the project; Robert Mackwood, our literary agent, who introduced this work to the publishers; and Doug Pepper of Signal/McClelland & Stewart (Penguin Random House Canada) who brought it to life.

David Johnston
Ottawa 2016

HIS EXCELLENCY THE RIGHT HONOURABLE DAVID JOHNSTON, GOVERNOR GENERAL OF CANADA

The 28th Governor General of Canada, His Excellency the Right Honourable David Johnston's life has been in public service. A strong believer in both equality of opportunity and excellence, His Excellency spent most of his career in higher education as a professor and later administrator of several of Canada's leading universities. His Excellency has focused his mandate on a vision of a smarter and more caring nation by reinforcing learning and innovation, encouraging philanthropy and volunteerism, and supporting families and children. Since his installation as governor general in October 2010, Mr. Johnston has travelled widely across Canada and around the world, connecting, honouring and inspiring Canadians and their global partners.